BRASS
TRIUMPHANT

BRASS TRIUMPHANT

Cyril Bainbridge

FREDERICK MULLER LIMITED
LONDON

First published in Great Britain 1980
by Frederick Muller Limited, London, NW2 6LE
Copyright © 1980 Cyril Bainbridge

British Library Cataloguing in Publication Data
Bainbridge, Cyril
    Brass triumphant.
    1. Bands (Music) – Great Britain
    I. Title
    785'.06'71   ML1331
ISBN 0 584 10372 7

Printed in Great Britain by The Anchor Press Ltd, and
bound by Wm. Brendon & Son Ltd, both of Tiptree, Essex

(Dedication)

To the memory of my father, who introduced me to brass bands.

CONTENTS

List of Photographs

Acknowledgements

Many people have assisted me in different ways in the preparation of this book. I would like to thank the many band officials, conductors, and others who have unhesitatingly given their time to me in interviews or in correspondence answering my enquiries. I am particularly grateful to Miss Imogen Holst for permission to quote from her book *The Music of Gustav Holst*; to J. M. Dent and Sons Ltd for permission to quote from *The Brass Band Movement* by J. F. Russell and J. H. Elliott; to the Editor of *The Times* for allowing the use of extracts from that paper; and to the Editors of *Brass Band News* and *The British Bandsman* for permission to use quotations from their publications. I was also very fortunate to talk to Captain Jenty Fairbank and Major Norman Bearcroft about the Salvation Army bands.

My thanks are also due to my daughter, Miss Mandy Bainbridge, who assisted in checking the manuscript and made a number of helpful suggestions, and to my elder daughter, Mrs Susan O'Sullivan, and to Mrs Evelyn Merritt, who typed the manuscript. The Editor of *The Times* has also allowed me to use a number of photographs by staff photographers: other pictures are from my own collection. Finally, I must express gratitude to my wife, Barbara, for her interest and forbearance throughout my involvement in researching and writing the book, and to my publishers for their helpfulness at all times.

Introduction

Brass banding is a pastime pursued among its players and supporters with as much zeal as the game of professional football. Indeed, footballing metaphors abound among bandsmen and many analogies are drawn with that sport. There are similar promotions and relegations between the various sections of competitive banding, and the national championships have area qualifying rounds separated into four divisions. The finals in London every year have much of the atmosphere of a Wembley Cup Final; the Royal Albert Hall, where the champions in Division One perform, is dominated by banners and a silver trophy which is not dissimilar in appearance to the F.A. Cup. The champion bands have their star performers; there is a tremendous team spirit in the bands; there are the supporters to cheer them on; and sometimes there is the disappointment of a bad performance resulting in the favourites being toppled. Players and conducters change bands with the frequency of transferred footballers and club managers in the sporting field, although the fees involved are vastly lower.

The competitive element in brass banding has provided the life-blood of the movement throughout its history, from the earliest days more than 150 years ago when bands were formed to provide an activity for workmen at a time when there was little opportunity for leisure pursuits. Some of the great rivalries of that period are still evident today.

A roll call of brass bands is like an evocation of industrial and social history, the changing titles illustrating the shifting patterns of life. The movement's origins as a significant manifestation of working-class culture have given it an image which is now outmoded. Most people, quite wrongly, still associate brass bands with cloth-capped working men from Yorkshire mills and mines,

1

capable of playing only marches and simple arrangements of light operatic music. Throughout its history the classical musical profession has been condescending to brass bands, to say the least. The result is that until the last few decades brass bands led an isolated existence, although they have always had a large and widespread following of devotees. Even in the 1860s in London, when brass bands were primarily centred in the north of the country, there were audiences of nearly 30,000 over a two-day festival. The cloth-cap image was cast aside years ago: it is now a classless movement with lawyers and tax inspectors, professional men and plumbers, managers and millhands and miners sitting together to enjoy their music-making. Brass bandsmen have proved that their musical pursuits are not a casual sideline, but that the movement is a serious musical medium. The extension of its repertoire through difficult test-pieces or, more recently, *avant-garde* music has shown the bandsmens' musicianship to be equal to the demands of this untraditional music.

The musical ability and artistry of these amateur musicians has often astonished distinguished members of the orchestral establishment and inspired them to contribute to the expanding repertoire. The movement's emergence into the wider musical sphere has led to the appearance of brass bands at many of the major music festivals and at Promenade Concerts.

Brass bands in America and Canada are not equivalent to the British phenomena. So-called brass bands in the United States have a construction more akin to the military band, with its use of woodwind and brass instruments. Mr André Previn, the orchestral conductor, who has a healthy respect for British brass bands, has, however, started an appreciation society in the United States for the British type of band. In Europe, close contacts have been established, often with the assistance of leading British instrument manufacturers such as Boosey & Hawkes, and there is now a thriving British-style brass band movement in many European countries. This development has recently been further encouraged by the addition of European championships held in London on the day following the national championships. Invariably, in these countries where such developments have taken place, national organizations have been created to co-ordinate the activities of the growing number of brass bands. It is, however, ironic that in Britain the musical artistry of brass bandsmen is not usually matched by similar administrative abilities; they have displayed a scepticism of central organization that has resulted in the failure of all attempts to introduce a national organization in the movement. Accordingly, there are no accurate figures of the numbers of either bands or bandsmen: only estimates of about 3,000 bands and 100,000 bandsmen.

Bandsmen are conservative in outlook, slow to accept change – it has taken, for example, almost 150 years for percussion to be permitted in contests. Nevertheless, the brass band movement has undergone a *renaissance* in recent years, due to several factors.

Although patronage of brass bands is not a new phenomenon – the earliest bands often had the financial support of an employer or colliery owner – in the last few decades sponsorship by commercial concerns has rapidly extended in this and other areas of the movement, such as the organization of contests. Other significant developments have been the addition of women players and conductors in what has traditionally been a predominantly male activity, the encouragement of brass bands through school and youth bands (with their own organizations and contests), many of which have established close links with bands overseas, a widening of the brass band audience, and the writing of good contemporary music.

Despite its strong tendency to cling to many of its obsolete traditions, it is a progressive movement which has successfully captured the interest of young players and, therefore, secured its future.

Chapter One

Beginnings

Brass bands have a long history with origins in the old waits, or town bands, of medieval times, the later church bands, military and circus bands, and wind bands. But it was the social and economic conditions of the early and mid-nineteenth century which were conducive to the evolution of brass bands and which nurtured their growth and immensely valuable contribution to a thriving musical life in provincial Britain. This was a period in which there was noticeable emulation in music-making, although the diverse sections 'of musical life tended to remain largely self-contained. The so-called upper classes of society had music salons in their town houses and country estates, which were emulated by the middle classes with musical evenings and with strong support of subscription concerts and choral music. The workers, often encouraged by enlightened and sometimes altruistic employers, copied their superiors by seizing the opportunity, provided through one of the new works bands or at the then increasing number of Mechanics' Institutes, to learn to play a brass instrument.

Mechanics' Institutes did not only teach the playing of instruments but often formed their own bands. This same period also, happily, coincided with technical advances in the construction of musical instruments, particularly the invention of the cornet-à-piston, which made manipulation and mastery of the instrument easier than was the case with, for instance, woodwind instruments. The introduction of the piston on the cornet and other instruments transferred the strain of playing from the throat and lips to the hands which, in the case of workmen, were often rough from the performance of their work but nevertheless dextrous. The fact that instruments were operated by the fingering of three valves made it possible for performers to be taught in class, and for a man who either became proficient at or disliked one instrument to be transferred with little difficulty to another.

This new musical enthusiasm, encouraged in many instances because of its moral qualities, had earlier shown itself in a choral form which, like the brass band movement that was to surge forward in the middle of the century, had a strong competitive character about it. Brass and voices have been brought into unison in music-making over the years. Both are mainly amateur forms of musical expression; both have strong north country traditions. Even today bands like the Black Dyke Mills Band and choirs such as Huddersfield Choral Society, both famous for their particular form of music, often perform together, particularly in Christmas carol concerts, and have recorded selections of festive music. And, of course, one has to go no further than the nearest Salvation Army citadel to hear fine music and singing regularly performed by a combination of band and songsters.

The waits from which brass bands are descended have a history of at least 500 years. They were originally watchmen in palaces, castles and walled towns who, at intervals, piped watch on a musical instrument to change the guard, to raise the alarm, or to act as a human alarm clock to awaken dignitaries by performing soft music outside their chamber doors. Local records show that they were paid a fee or granted tenure of land for their services. It was a period in which there were large numbers of wandering minstrels and the waits jealously guarded their superior positions as employees of royalty, the nobility or municipalities.

An act of Elizabeth I classed all wandering minstrels as 'rogues, vagabonds and sturdy beggars' and required itinerant musicians to wear cloaks and badges of their patrons to denote whom they served – the Ruritanian gold-braided uniforms of modern bandsmen are a legacy of those times. Persecution caused many of the nomadic minstrels to settle down. They banded together in guilds to protect their interests and thus many waits were formed. Their duties were extended to assisting in the performance of medieval plays, by serenading notable visitors and playing along the routes of royal visitors – another ancient duty which is still performed by twentieth-century bandsmen.

The waits were disbanded as a result of the Municipal Reform Act of 1835. In fact, most had been dismissed earlier because of the economic difficulties created by the Napoleonic Wars, although in a few instances the custom of playing in the streets at Advent and Christmas survived for some years: the playing of carols at Christmas is still a feature of brass bands.

Many of the waits continued to perform in church bands. Before the mid-seventeenth century, church music had been provided by organs but these instruments were forbidden by the Puritans. An ordinance of 1644 decreed that 'all Organs, and the Frames and Cases wherein they stand in all Churches and or Chapels aforesaid, shall be taken away and utterly defaced and none hereafter set up in their places'. The help of vocalists and instrumentalists was sought to fill the gap. Many of the local people had been taught to play various instruments by itinerant professional musicians from the theatres in taverns and ale-houses; they taught quickly, and enthusiastic amateur musicians added to the nucleus of church bandsmen. The bands usually numbered half a dozen instrumentalists and were accommodated in the choir gallery. Their leader was usually the parish clerk.

Their music-making was not always entirely confined to the sacred music of the church. In some instances the bands also doubled-up as rural orchestras or even performed as dance bands. Thomas Hardy, the Wessex novelist, has recorded an authentic and entertaining account of the multifarious activities of the church band. Hardy acquired considerable experience of church music and bands from his father and other close relatives who were the mainstay of the church band at Stinsford in Devon. As a youth Hardy had even contemplated ordination and the experience of his close relatives, coupled with his own as a noted fiddler at local functions, provided him with the factual background for the musical episodes in his novels. The Mellstock church band, which is portrayed in *Under the Greenwood Tree*, came into dispute with their vicar over their banishment and their substitution with an organ, and provided Hardy with one of the main strands of his novel. Hardy, despite his later agnostic stand, retained throughout his life a considerable regard for church music and regretted the ultimate passing of the church band.

Throughout the country church bands were beginning to suffer a fate similar to that of the Mellstock players, despite their having flourished for many years. Ironically, the advent of the harmonium or American organ displaced them. There was the occasional exception. At Winterborne Abbas in Hardy's native Dorset, for example, the church band managed to survive the changing pattern until almost the end of the century: it was not until about 1896 that it was finally replaced in that particular outpost. There were also faint echoes of the waits elsewhere. In 1895 Daniel Hardman, who, over 60 years earlier had assisted in the formation of an amateur brass band at York was still alive, the sole survivor of a City Wait for which he was still in receipt of a pension of £2.10s. (£2.50). Church bands, particularly in rural areas, and the town bands in the expanding urban districts had, in their respective ways, been the bellows through which the breath of life had been instilled into music in provincial England.

Brass bands were often associated with churches or other religious groups. Here are two examples: *above* Banbury (Oxon) Wesleyan Mission Band, photographed in 1908, and *below* Christ Church Band from Leyton in north-east London.

The whole pattern of life, however, was changing rapidly as a result of the development of the country from a predominantly rural and agricultural community into an industrialized urban environment. The close community that characterized rural and village life, with the paternalism of squire and farmer, was being replaced in the rapidly growing towns, created from the Industrial Revolution, by a largely uncared for community of artisans: uncared for, that is, in terms of social and leisure compensations. The rural worker had for his enjoyment the long-standing traditional amusements such as games on the village green, harvest suppers, feasts and field sports and May Day festivities. In the towns such leisure amusements were missing, although May Day festivities later took on a political connotation in the industrial towns and cities. In contrast to the close rural community, the towns were peopled by much larger groups; hundreds of people worked together in the factories and mills compared to the half dozen hands on the farm. The mill-owner, too, was often far more remote than the farmer and the squire in the country. The town dweller, then, had to look elsewhere for his sport. Evangelical religion, non-conformism and radical politics filled the gap. They were 'tinder to the flame of agitation'.* Drink was the only luxury, an escape from the primitive home surroundings and the often repetitive nature of their employment, whether in factory or mine.

The period between the great Reform Bills of 1832 and 1867 – a period which saw the birth of the railway and the development of the country's mineral resources – is undoubtedly one of the most interesting of Britain's entire history. The population was increasing rapidly and the main source of its wealth was shifting from agriculture to industry: the census of 1851 showed that half the population by then was urban. Industrial change was having significant social effects. The wealth created from industrial growth was raising the wages of large sections of the working classes. Skilled engineers became the élite of the workers. They and other craftsmen created an aristocracy of their own and formed trade unions and guilds to protect their position and further improve their remuneration.

Meanwhile, other less privileged sections were suffering hard times and exploitation which, particularly in the north of England, led to fierce agitation among factory workers. There was felt to be a need to direct some of this energy into calmer fields and this manifested itself in the development of educational and recrea-

---

*G. M. Trevelyan, *English Social History* (Longman)

tional pursuits for the working classes, encouraged and financially supported by factory and colliery owners. The skilled workers and craftsmen, the more intelligent section of the working class population, sought to improve themselves culturally as well as materially. The opportunity was provided through the introduction of ventures like the Mechanics' Institutes, which began in Scotland in 1823, the brainchild of Dr George Birkbeck, a Yorkshireman whose name is perpetuated in the college which forms part of London University. The venture quickly spread to England. Two hundred institutes had been established by 1841 and 20 years later there were 750, mostly in the Midlands, Yorkshire and Lancashire. Lord Brougham became associated with the movement's expansion in England and the Institute manual, published over his signature in 1839, argued that the lack of amusement drove men into vice and criminal activities and that if they were to become useful, active and contented members of society, recreation was an urgent necessity. Music was therefore included in the curriculum to utilize any excesses of energy that might otherwise have been expended in riot and debauchery.

The disappearance of the waits had almost coincided with the first of the brass bands, although they were then combinations of wind and reed instruments. They did not become entirely brass until the 1830s and 1840s. Two of the best known bands which are still in the top league of brass bands started in this way. Black Dyke Mills Band, as it is now universally known, began its existence in around 1816 in the high West Yorkshire village of Queensbury, near Bradford, as a brass and reed band, then known as Peter Wharton's Band. One of the players was John Foster, a local mill-owner and enthusiastic amateur musician. When the original band became threatened with extinction Foster attached it to his works under its present title and it became a wholly brass band at the same time. Similarly, over the border in Lancashire, Besses o' th' Barn Band began its existence two years after Black Dyke in 1818: it was then known as Clegg's Reed Band. With a similar composition it later became Besses Military Band until in 1849, and with the unusually small number, by modern comparison, of only nine players, it changed to an all-brass-band. Another early example of this mixture of reed and brass was at Stalybridge, a mill town on the Lancashire-Cheshire border. From 1809 onwards efforts were made to organize a band which finally succeeded in the setting up of Stalybridge Old Band in 1814. The reed instruments were eliminated in the 1840s in the general movement to all-brass combinations.

There is much competition for the distinction of being the earliest band. Apart from those mentioned above, another of the earliest bands and almost certainly the first example of a colliery band was the Coxlodge Band which dates back to 1809 when a Mr Tuiton and some employees of the Burradon and Coxlodge Coal Company of Newcastle-on-Tyne formed an amateur brass band. 'As far as can be ascertained that was the beginning of the brass band movement in this country,' claimed a writer in the industrial magazine *Coal* in 1948.

In Wales, however, it is claimed there was a band at Blaina (now part of Gwent) in 1805. But, says Gwyn M. Jones, secretary of the existing Blaina band, there has never been any record of its formation or of its form. It may, he says, have been just a few enthusiasts using some home-made instruments to produce some kind of noise. Blaina lays justified claim to being the first all-brass band however. The present band in Blaina owes its origins to the Brown's Works Band, which was also a brass and reed ensemble, centred around the local iron works. In 1817 its conductor was Karl Schaeffer, a German employed at the works. During a discussion with another German friend, a traveller, Schaeffer decided he would like to form an all-brass ensemble, then a complete innovation in Britain, and persuaded his employers to provide the finance necessary to buy a set of brass instruments, which was imported from Amsterdam.

It is from this decision in 1817 that Blaina has always claimed to be the oldest all-brass band in Great Britain, says Gwyn Jones. Some of the original brass instruments were still in use as late as 1929. From Brown's Works Band there developed the Blaina Lancaster Band, Blaina Town Band, Blaina Youth Band and, currently, Blaina and District Silver Band. This village band had a meteoric rise from the fourth to the championship section, but Jones explains, it was neither financially nor administratively strong enough to cope with the problems involved in that standard of banding and there was genuine regret in 1978 at reports that the band had been dissolved. However, as is so often the case, a few enthusiasts have throughout the difficulties tried to keep the band afloat and they are hopeful of its eventual return to the contesting stage. Unfortunately, all documents relating to the band's history were destroyed in a fire over 40 years ago: who has the rightful claim to being the first band to be formed may never be satisfactorily resolved. In Scotland, Langholm Town Band claims to have been formed around 1815 and Airdrie Union Band was in existence at about the same period. Which band is the oldest is of academic interest only today. Some of the early contenders have fallen on hard times and disappeared from the brass band scene; they were in any case not strictly brass bands. What is more important is the fact that many of those early bands have survived various vicissitudes and are still in existence without a break in their continuity.

The era which saw the birth of brass bands was a grim period in British history which had important social effects. From 1793 until 1815 Great Britain had been almost continuously at war with France, a period that was not only lengthy but expensive and one that had serious effects on the economy and the morale of its citizens for many years after the war had ended.

The needs of the war effort had accelerated the introduction of steam power and machinery in industry. The introduction of the new machines threatened the livelihood of cottage workers and in many instances brought a new way of life. Some of the resistance to the march of industrial progress manifested itself in the Luddite riots of 1812 when stocking machines in Nottinghamshire were smashed. Similar incidents followed in Yorkshire and Lancashire.

The post-war years were marked by riots, strikes, campaigns for reform, government repression, industrial depression, bad harvests and discontent over the great changes in agriculture and industry. More immediately there were the results on the industrial employment scene of demobilization and the decline of those industries that had become prosperous as a result of the wars. By the 1830s, however, the scene was beginning to change. Exports were increasing, as were wages in many areas of industry. In those areas in which brass bands were nurtured, demand for cotton and cloth was on the increase and a series of inventions such as the flying shuttle, mule spinning and the Spinning Jenny had revolutionized techniques and were changing the traditional cottage industries to a factory base.

Even in 1830, though, there were estimated to be about 200,000 handlooms still at work in the cotton industry and it was not until about the middle of the century that there was widespread use of the power loom in the woollen textile industry..One of the main reasons for the decline of the textile industry in East Anglia and the West Country was that demand during the wars for the coarser materials manufactured in the West Riding increased. The decline was made absolute with the introduction of power-driven machinery: the access of areas around Manchester and the West

Riding to the rich coalfields gave them overwhelming advantages over their East Anglian and West Country competitors.

As these areas developed into the great centres of the cotton and woollen industries, tremendous and complex social implications resulted: slums and overcrowding in the home environment were combined with unhealthy and dangerous conditions in the badly ventilated, barrack-like factories in which workers spent long hours. They also had to contend with a rigid discipline in the factories with, in some cases, fines being imposed for such heinous 'offences' as leaving factory windows open to admit fresh air or for singing at work. Such were the atmosphere and conditions into which brass bands were born.

While great scientific and technological advances were being made in industrial developments, experimentation was also going on in the field of musical instruments which was to have a profound effect. With the exception of the drum, primitive musical instruments were invariably those developed from a hollow animal horn from which music was obtained through the input of breath. Reed instruments developed quickly from these primitive beginnings, but the reed bands began to lose their appeal when wind instruments such as the bassoon and horn were developed. Trombones had already been in use for some years, forming part of the complement of waits and church bands.

Much of the inventiveness in musical instruments before this period had originated in Germany and had been introduced into Britain through military bands, which were often led by German or Italian bandmasters. The drum, the trumpet and the horn had traditionally been used to revive the flagging spirits of marching troops and to stimulate their emotions as they went into battle. The French, too, emulating the enthusiastic Germans, also played a part in spreading the interest to Britain, largely through Charles II who, when he returned to the English throne from his exile in France, brought a strong influence from that country into his martial music. Known then as the sackbut, the trombone, which had been used in royal bands at the time of Henry VIII and subsequently in the waits and church bands, had been introduced into military bands towards the end of the eighteenth century. In the early years of the nineteenth century, however, new instruments such as the bassoon, horn and clarinet were being introduced and wind bands became for a time a popular form of music-making.

One of the earliest of British inventions was that of James Halliday who, in 1810, developed a chromatic bugle horn by putting valves or keys along its length, an innovation which opened up immense possibilities for the future of brass bands, as well as pre-empting some other European countries where similar research was being undertaken. Halliday's contribution has been described as the beginning of a positive progression.

This was followed in 1824 by another important advance in musical instrumentation from the unlikely source of a Derbyshire farmer-cum-inventor: John Shaw, of Glossop, in that year took out a patent for a spring slide which could be used on a variety of instruments. They were of two varieties: in one the pressure on the slide made the tone sharper; in the other the pressure on the slide lowered or flattened the tone of the instrument. For three years Shaw continued his experiments, constructing a trumpet he described as having 'four clean button-top pistoned upright valves, having singular connecting tops and lower and slide tubes to each valve'.

Shaw had spent 17 years altogether experimenting with his valves, producing during that time five original valves. The brass band movement's indebtedness to him is enormous, but as so often happened in those days he gained little financial reward for his labours. There was then no international agreement to restrict the copying of patents and, while he worked at improvements on his invention, others were copying his original patented valve, both in Britain and abroad. An Amsterdam instrument-maker, Embach, introduced the cornopean in 1830, a more compact development of Shaw's instrument which he turned into a more manageable proposition by reducing the valves from four to three. In Britain, too, others were improving on Shaw's original invention. Wigglesworth's, a firm of instrument makers at Otley, in the Wharfe Valley of West Yorkshire, were producing their own version and selling it to most of the bands that were then beginning to come into existence in Yorkshire, a county which was fast becoming one of the main nurseries of brass bands.

The Distins, a talented family of brass instrumentalists, at around this period played an important part in popularizing concerted brass performances through extensive concert tours which they undertook in Britain and abroad. The head of the family, John Distin, who was born in 1798, had had an interesting musical career. He had been a band boy in the South Devon Militia and was so accomplished a performer that at the age of 14 he played principal trumpet in performances of Handel's *Dettinger Te Deum*. At 16 he became solo bugler with the Grenadier Guards Band. He later encouraged his four sons to play musical instruments and as they grew up they formed a family ensemble of brass instrumentalists.

It was during a visit to Paris that Distin first heard the saxhorn, the invention of Adolph Sax. Such was Distin's enthusiasm for the new instrument that he immediately ordered five for his family band. They performed on them in 1844 at a concert promoted by the composer Berlioz: the instrument was an immediate success and Distin introduced it to England the following year. It was a move which helped in encouraging the formation of amateur brass bands. The instruments patented by Sax with the piston principle proved popular with both the public, for their tonal quality, and with players for what Enderby Jackson, a pioneer of the brass band movement whose work will be referred to later, described as their 'full and free power and good intonation and, more especially, for their ease in blowing and simple fingering'. It was this latter quality that was such a significant factor since most of the members of brass bands came from the 'weekly wage earning classes ... Their hands, horned and often malformed by their daily toil, were well served in these new instruments by the short, easy manipulation, three fingers sufficing to work the mechanism of the three equi-distant pistons'.

The early Victorian era was marked by industrial progress, which brought some slight reduction in working hours, better pay and holidays for many. But most people in the heavy industrial areas continued to live in a drab environment in which they had to content themselves with the simplest of pleasures. Life inevitably centred around the public houses, which became the local cultural focus for these deprived people. The music in their life derived mainly from the singing saloons in the public houses. Sociologically, this situation resulted in two important developments – one direct, the other indirect – in the musical life of Britain. It was in these saloons that the music hall was born: the indirect contribution lay in the expanding temperance movement, strongly supported by enlightened employers who, for various motives, sought to keep their operatives from the dangers of alcohol. The temperance movement took some time to get into its stride but by the 1830s it was beginning to assume some significance. In order to do so it had adopted a somewhat aggressive approach to its endeavours, similar to the later evangelism of the Salvation Army, and what better way to draw attention to its message and activities than by the strident music of the brass band.

In some instances the twin talents of voice and brass combined in the public houses. In the 1860s for instance it is recorded that the Old Cock Inn in Preston had 'excellent singing and a brass band'. It is not clear whether the public house had its own brass band or whether a local band hired a room there in which to practise, as many bands did, with the customers joining in the refrains.

The temperance movement resulted in the creation of many brass bands to lead campaigning throughout Britain against the evils of drink. Bramley Old Band, near Leeds, which came to life in 1828 as a reed band, was reorganized in 1836 and became the first temperance brass band to be established in England. Some of these denominational bands, like the Wingates Temperance Band from Lancashire, are still in existence and have retained their titles even in these less prohibitive times. Another of the leading bands, Brighouse and Rastrick, at one time was also a temperance band but subsequently this definition was removed from its title.

Nunhead Christian Band from south east London in 1913. The band had been formed 17 years earlier. "We are all abstainers and non-smokers and enforce the rule of 'One man, one band,' wrote the Bandmaster, Mr. H. Leggett.

Many of the smaller local bands which were a by-product of the temperance movement found themselves in decline in succeeding years as the movement itself became less of a force; others found their bandsmen, thirsty after a practice or an engagement, succumbed to the temptation to refresh themselves with the local brew. Often a band remained in existence but dispensed with the temperance label.

In some instances, the setting up of a temperance band prompted intense local rivalries. An example was at Wyke, then a village near Bradford, West Yorkshire, where the establishment of a new temperance band in 1869 led to clashes with supporters of the longer established Wyke Old Band, and virtually divided the villagers. Their rivalry extended to the contest arena and, when the bands had competed against each other, supporters of both would gather in the village street for their return, eagerly awaiting the strains of a particular tune which signified which of the two had been victorious. By 1888, when the Old Band disbanded, the temperance band was among the leading bands of the day and had succeeded in winning more than £1,200, a sizeable sum in those days, in prize money. It continued its existence into the turn of the century but the temperance label was dropped in its latter years.

Whatever they did for the temperance movement, there is no doubt about the contribution of these bands towards widening musical knowledge and creating interest in brass bands. The Leeds Temperance Band, for example, in 1847 was invited for a fee of £60 to undertake a summer season of four weeks' duration playing for holiday-makers at Scarborough, an engagement that proved to be so popular and successful that they were invited again for the two following years.

Religion also played a part in the development of music. Church bands, as we have seen, provided an important thread in the brass band fabric. The non-conformist religions later made their own contribution by impressing the moral qualities of music and music-making. Many new bands around the middle of the century were formed among Sunday schools, missions and other religious institutions, but records show that these attachments were often quickly broken – as they were in the case of the temperance bands – for a more independent existence. Although various religious denominations made a contribution, the Methodists in particular encouraged hymn singing and enthusiastically elevated music in their services. George Hogarth in 1838 summed up the musical scene in the industrial north: 'In the densely peopled manufacturing districts of Yorkshire, Lancashire and Derbyshire, music is cultivated among the working classes to an extent unparalleled in any other part of the kingdom. Every town has its choral society, supported by amateurs of the place and its neighbourhood, where the sacred works of Handel and the more modern masters are performed with precision and effect by a voice and instrumental orchestra consisting of mechanics and work people; every village church has its occasional holiday oratorio.' It is a situation that has not changed much in those same areas in the intervening years, despite the modern diversions of radio and television.

The mill-worker may have had little to sing about during his working hours and, as we have seen, the cramped home conditions drove many to find their pleasures after work elsewhere than around the home. Fortunately for music not all of them resorted to the public houses. This was the period in which choral societies sprang into life in many towns and villages for the simple reason that it did not cost anything to make vocal music. It was only a few years later that brass bands began to proliferate as a little more money became available among these same artisans, enabling them to buy instruments or subscribe towards a band if listening to music, rather than making it, was their forte. There were also instances of mutual help in the purchase of instruments.

New developments in instrument manufacture simplified the playing of brass instruments and made players in a band interchangeable; and the extension of musical education to more people, and the desire of many factory-owners to direct the leisure energies of their workforce into more cultural and entertaining activities, were all factors which helped to advance the brass band. Two others were also to have a significant effect on the spread of brass bands and their increasing popularity. The first was the Great Exhibition of 1851. Workers from all over Britain attended the exhibition, often assisted by preferential fares and works outings. There the newly improved brass instruments, which many had heard used by performers such as the Distin family, were on the stands of the British and foreign manufacturers: in addition, talented players were there to demonstrate instruments, and hundreds if not thousands of visitors to the exhibition must have returned home resolving to take up one of these instruments. It was fortunate that the advances of technology had simplified the instruments; and hands, roughened through hard toil, which would have had difficulty with the delicate fingering of a violin, could more easily master the three valves of a cornet or other brass instrument.

The early growth of the brass band movement was stimulated by the rapid development of the railways. Cheap travel came within reach of large sections of the population: excursions to the seaside resorts, springing up in all manner of places as a result of the railway mania, were encouraged and there many were introduced to band concerts on the promenade or pier. Growth of the railways also produced a side-effect which was to become probably the most significant development in the history of brass bands. Cheaper fares meant that bands were able to become more mobile: to accept engagements over a wider area. Rivalry was ever present and when two or more bands met together challenges were likely to be issued. Full-scale brass band contests were the inevitable result. They became the life-blood of the brass band movement.

Cheap rail fares and sea excursions had an important social effect: they helped to bring about the development of many formerly quiet fishing villages into bustling seaside resorts, creating at the same time a new race of pleasure-seeking pilgrims. 'There are Canterbury pilgrims every Sunday in summer . . . who go by the South Eastern railway and come back the same day for five shillings,' Samuel Butler, the author and satirist, observed. 'If they don't go to Canterbury they go by the *Clacton Belle* to Clacton-on-Sea. There is not a Sunday the whole summer through but you may find all Chaucer's pilgrims on board the *Lord of the Isles* or the *Clacton Belle*.'

At the resort there was invariably a band – military or brass – performing for their entertainment on one of the ornate new bandstands. These were erected on the promenade or beneath oriental-like domes on one of the piers that were then beginning to extend their metallic tentacles out into the sea.

Many of the excursions were works trips or Sunday School outings on which music and singing formed a vital part of the day's jollity and entertainment. Sometimes the trippers would be accompanied by their own band, like the occasion in 1844 when a Preston factory owner paid for 650 of his employees, accompanied by 70 friends and acquaintances, to go on a pleasure trip to Fleetwood. They started out early in the morning, assembling in the factory yard, and marched in procession to the railway station with a Church of England band at their head.

Bands were often engaged to lead children's outings, mainly to keep up the flagging spirits of the youngsters as they marched to or from the station. The martial music of the band, the hissing of steam from the massive, mystical engine, the whistle of the train – all are nostalgic recollections of these past occasions. Advertisements proclaimed the engagement of 'two powerful bands' as part of the inducement to travel by train for one of these grand seaside picnics. The general superintendent of one railway company, quoting terms to an excursion organizer, said members of a band, if in uniform, would be carried at half the quoted fare of 4s. (20p).

It was perhaps fortuitous that the railways were more advanced in the north of England where brass bands were at their strongest in both numbers and support. In turn, the contests they were able to travel to created further interest in and expansion of the brass band movement.

The increasing availability of leisure activities such as excursions and music and singing was not always matched by an increase in leisure time in which to pursue them. Half-days off on Saturday were still the exception rather than the rule. This meant so far as singers and musicians were concerned that only Sundays were available for concerts and other performances.

There had even then been a long tradition of outdoor music in public places. The pleasure gardens of London were the models for public concerts in parks which were becoming a popular form of summer Sunday afternoon entertainment, but which in latter years have sadly declined due to changes in musical taste and financial economies by local councils. But the pleasure gardens of the early eighteenth century also have an important place in the history of music, although music often formed only a part of the entire programme. The 'orchestra' was frequently built around the other forms of entertainment provided. In some instances, resident composers were employed and they provided a repertoire of stirring, patriotic marches and other music, much of which Edward Baines, a Leeds Member of Parliament, had in mind when he resisted what he believed to be the potential onslaught on the Sabbath that band concerts in the parks presented.

Brass bands gave, in the main, open air performances – programmes in the parks, local fêtes and galas, Sunday School treats and, indeed, in almost any form of outdoor activity. This created a dilemma, particularly for the non-conformists who, on the one hand, encouraged musical activities for their moral value yet, on the other, were prejudiced against musical performances on the Sabbath for secular purposes. Edward Baines seriously believed music in the parks would invite civil disobedience. 'The love of music is all but universal', he wrote in a pamphlet. 'In itself it is innocent and lawful but it may be used for the worst purposes, as well as for the best. The strains of martial music cause the pulse to bound and fire the imagination, and they are wholly out of accord with the sacred repose of the Sabbath.'

That brass bands sometimes did attract disreputable elements is undeniable although as in many other respects through the ages it was abuse by a minority that led to their condemnation. Socially, however, there was much in their favour. Social distinctions were not generally apparent and they certainly introduced to the masses forms of music which would not otherwise have been available, a factor which can only have been to the advantage of both the music and those who listened to it. Much of the music consisted at this time of selections from the opera and oratorio, but such concerts also provided a platform for new composers, many of whom could be seen personally performing their works.

Outdoor concerts were undoubtedly an extremely popular form of public entertainment which, not surprisingly, inevitably spread to other parts of the country. Many of the larger centres of population copied the London pleasure gardens format: Birmingham had its own equivalent of Vauxhall Gardens, Newcastle promoted weekly garden concerts, and Norwich at one time boasted three pleasure gardens. And the spas, by then frequented not only by rich hypochondriacs but also by those in search of the lively social life that had been built up in these health centres, largely through the patronage of the newly rich created by the industrial expansion, were all providing indoor and outdoor musical programmes, engaging bands for weekly periods to give up to three performances daily.

Whatever the pros and cons, Sunday band music became a contentious issue in the Victorian period. Its sheer popularity, however, could not easily be overlooked and was an influencing factor in overcoming the bigotry and controversy it created. Numerically, the supporters outweighed the opponents. As many as 20,000 people attended Sunday band concerts on Bristol Downs, for instance. A committee set up in that city to contest the opponents of Sunday music argued that it was 'breaking no law, human or divine, in providing innocent recreation for many thousands of all classes'. The objectors, if not immediately silenced, were subdued.

Edward Baines was right about one thing: there can be no doubt that the strident tones of martial music have the effect of stirring the adrenalin. The music of military bands had for years been recognized as a stimulant both to soldiers going into battle or those on the march, a recognition which manifested itself in the large number of regimental bands, many of which remain to this day despite curtailment in both defence manpower and finance. Throughout the history of the brass band movement there has always been a strong affinity between the two types of band and many players have given long service in one or other or both.

Part of this particularly close relationship can be attributed to the creation in 1859 of the Volunteer movement. Napoleon III's intentions caused much concern and resulted in the Volunteers, a force in which factory-owners and their employees trained to combat any evil threat from across the Channel.

The marching and drilling had to be accompanied by martial music, resulting in the formation of a network of Volunteer brass bands over the whole country but which was particularly strong in Yorkshire, Lancashire, the Midlands and Scotland. It was mainly from the Volunteer movement that brass bands were nurtured in Scotland. They were also formed further south and a London Volunteer Corps band stormed Belle Vue, the great northern citadel of the brass band world, and carried off second prize in the championships of 1861. Some of these bands subsequently became full military bands, while in other instances they were converted into independent bands or town bands when players found the military discipline demanded of them too restrictive. Lewes Town Band started out as the Lewes Town and Volunteer Cinque Ports Band and for many years executed a duty that had previously been performed by military bands stationed in the vicinity – the provision of two men to play trumpets as heralds at the Sussex Assizes held in the town. Directly and indirectly, the Volunteer movement was responsible for the formation of a large number of bands and a further significant advance in the overall growth of the brass band movement.

The changeover to all-brass bands, thanks to advances in instrument technology, began to take effect in the 1830s and 1840s: it was the beginning of the climb to the peaks of popularity.Enthusiasm for brass built up among both potential players and supporters. It was an enthusiasm that in many instances infected industrialists who provided generous support. The provision of recreational facilities was becoming an important part of industrial welfare; bands featured prominently in this provision, along with sports clubs, flower shows and gardening societies, for example. This paternalism had been evident in some cases from the late eighteenth and nineteenth centuries and took many forms. From about 1750 in the northern districts of the Pennines, within a triangle formed by the towns of Hexham, Penrith and Darlington, a large population began to grow up engaged in the mining and smelting of lead. As the company, the London (Quaker) Lead Company, expanded its activities, hamlets were extended and in 1760 the company created a new village called Nent Head and made it virtually self-sufficient with the

Brass Bands had become numerous in the south of England by the turn of the century. Here are Northfleet (Kent) Band, *above* which celebrated its centenary in 1978, pictured in 1904, and *below* Barnet Town Prize Band in 1910 (a band is still in existence there, too).

provision of all the necessary social services. By the end of the century the company's activities in that area had drawn together a community of 4,000 people who were directly dependent on the company for their livelihood and leisure activities. Officials of this company were pioneers in both educational and recreational activities – even in the organization of working hours that enabled the miners to take advantage of the facilities.

Bands, of course, featured prominently, and the company made annual donations and subscribed towards the acquisition or replacement of instruments. One of the first of these bands was set up in the village of Nent Head in about 1820 and by 1835 there were bands in eight other villages where the company had an interest. Sometimes, in addition to new instruments, grants were made towards 'the dresses of the band'. The bands became a prominent feature of village life, playing at all the local shows and other occasions into the twentieth century, until the company went into liquidation in 1905.

Black Dyke Mills Band was taken under the wing of the textile firm of John Foster & Son – the largest mohair material manufacturers in the world – in the high West Yorkshire village of Queensbury in the 1850s, thanks to the fact that John Foster was himself a playing member. That support has been carried on up to the present time by successive generations of the family. Another supported band which achieved prominence in the competitive sphere in the last two decades of the nineteenth century was the Leeds Forge Band, formed in 1882 by Samson Fox, head of the company and a former mayor of Harrogate. He, too, equipped the band with instruments and uniforms, paid for their professional tuition and allowed generous absences from work for rehearsal and competitive engagements. Fox was equally generous in the wider musical world, being a benefactor of the Royal College of Music in London. Only a year after its formation, his works band was privileged to play at the opening of the college's new buildings in Prince Consort Road in 1883. Unlike Black Dyke Mills Band, though, the financial support for Leeds Forge Band was relatively short-lived. It petered out when there were changes in the management of the company in 1892. It had had a brilliant, if brief, career and the new directors must later have pondered on the wisdom of their decision to withdraw support in the light of the continued success of its contemporaries.

Sir Titus Salt, a Bradford manufacturer of alpaca cloth, was another great benefactor of social and leisure activities for his workforce. He built a complete town on the banks of the River Aire near Shipley, a few miles from Bradford, around his model factory. It provided for almost all the needs of his employees - housing, a hospital, church, meeting rooms and institute; everything they would require with the exception of a public house.

He took his own name and that of the river and called it Saltaire. The leisure facilities, of course, included a brass band. He paid for all the instruments and the tuition of the bandsmen: in return the bandsmen repaid his generosity with some notable successes in contests, for which they were further rewarded by their philanthropic employer in the form of bonuses. Sir Titus was renowned for his generosity. He entertained up to 4,000 of his employees at his home at Crow Nest, Lightcliffe, near Halifax, on special anniversaries. The Saltaire Band at that time was conducted by Richard Smith, one of the early pioneers of the movement. He was born at Batley in Yorkshire and later moved to Hull. He acquired a distinguished reputation as a professional trainer and conductor and was in much demand. He was also a prolific composer and eventually branched out into music publishing. He launched the *Champion Brass Band Journal* in 1857 which consisted of music for brass bands, and moved to London in 1878 where he set up a music publishing business which has kept pace with modern technology and still flourishes as publishers of brass band music and specialists in brass band recordings.

It is impossible to quantify in financial or other terms the benefits firms derived from the creation and support of works bands. In the early days it was seen as providing an antidote to the evils of drinking and helped alleviate the lack of recreation for the workforce. In some instances the philanthropic and good natured intentions of these industrial benefactors can be unquestioned: in others they were undoubtedly influenced by more ulterior motives and regarded their outlay as a hedge against industrial disruption at a time when there was considerable dissension over working and social conditions. This appears to have paid off since there were reported to be fewer strikes at factories where such facilities were provided.

Alongside the backing of an industrialist, which varied from the generous examples of total support from men such as John Foster and Samson Fox to provision of a room for practice, went the enthusiasm of non-playing workers and colleagues. A works band, particularly a successful one, invested a strong feeling of pride among the factory staff which is still evident today when fewer members of a band associated with a company may actually work for it.

Many of the other bands then being formed were less fortunate and had to rely upon the initial finance provided by members themselves for the purchase of their own instruments, until they were proficient enough to win some prize money. Another way of raising the necessary finance was in the form of subscriptions from both bandsmen and supporters.

Another of the oldest bands which still flourishes, Besses o' th' Barn, which for many years had the reputation of being the finest brass band in the country, was an independent band which built up its finances in this way, bolstered substantially by its income from successful contesting and the acceptance of engagements. Its finances were in such a healthy state during the 1880s that the bandsmen were able to buy their own building in November 1885 and set up a social club which, in turn, multiplied their original investment.

Besses o' th' Barn Band show off their trophies. In the centre is the extraordinary ornate Crystal Palace 1,000 guinea trophy which Besses won in 1903. To the right of the trophy stands Alexander Owen, the conductor who led them and many other famous bands to victory.

The temperance bands, mission bands, those associated with other religious groups, and many town bands, all of which were springing up in great profusion during the 1850s and 1860s, relied mainly on their sectional interests to keep them going, particularly by weekly subscriptions. They depended almost entirely on the small subscriptions and donations of bandsmen and their friends. Apart from Besses, the other most famous subscription band is the Brighouse and Rastrick Band. Salvation Army bands are also, in a sense, subscription bands since they too are supported from the small subscriptions of the musicians.

By the 1860s the brass band had become firmly established. The formation of new bands and the organization of contests were complementary and inseparable. A contemporary report commented: 'In all kinds of obscure places . . . brass bands struggled into existence. In days when forms of entertainment were limited and workers were compelled to explore their own resources in order to provide leisure-time interests, little stimulus was required to establish a band: membership provided at one stroke an outlet for surplus energy, an opportunity for congenial companionship and the prospect of titillating sport.'

The Victorian era was noted, among other things, for the do-it-yourself element in entertainment. Musical evenings around the piano in the parlour, which was invariably out of bounds except at weekends, were a feature of its leisure pursuits. This element of home-made musical entertainment in many instances resulted in several members of a family being members of a brass band. Father would encourage – perhaps teach – his son to play an instrument and as mastery of one instrument would result in easy transition to another, participation in brass band work became very much a family affair. There are countless examples of not only several members but several generations of a family playing together in the same band. A silver band at Bulkington, near Nuneaton, formed by Mr George Bicknell during the Crimean War included his five sons and was known locally as Bicknell's Band. Almost a century later the band was conducted by the founder's great-great grandson and still had seven members of the family among its players.

The one-time conductor of a British Legion Band at Oldham, Lancashire, started his career with the band as a boy, alongside his father and grandfather. Four members of another family and three of yet another all had long associations with the same band. A silver band at Hoo, near Rochester, Kent, was a truly family band: at one time its membership consisted of six members of the Simmons family, five of the Poynter family, three each from the Mathias and Peck families, and two each from the Beech and Lee families. In the case of another 'family' band, Joseph Levick, bandmaster in the 1950s of the Shirebrook Silver Prize Band from Mansfield, Nottinghamshire, had a son and grandson playing in the band, while there were also five examples of father and son among the players. Again in the 1950s Heage, Derbyshire, Silver

Band claimed a record by having six brothers in the band at the same time.

The most famous of brass band families must, however, be the Mortimer family whose various members have had extremely successful careers and have played dominant roles in brass band affairs during the present century. Fred Mortimer, born in 1879, began as a cornet player with Hebden Bridge Band in his native Yorkshire and became bandmaster in 1900. He later moved south to Luton whose band he conducted until 1924 when he moved to Fodens and with them twice achieved a hat trick in the Crystal Palace Championships and won once at Belle Vue, Manchester. His eldest son, Harry Mortimer, still playing a leading part in brass band affairs, was born in 1902 and began playing the cornet at the age of eight when the family was still at Hebden Bridge. He later played in the Luton Band with his two brothers, Alex and Rex, and went on to a distinguished career as principal cornet player with Fodens Band and helped them win the National Championships on 14 occasions. After playing with the Hallé, Liverpool Philharmonic and BBC Northern orchestras, his career continued as conductor of the Fairey Band and others, and as brass and military band adviser to the BBC. His two brothers also became well-known brass band conductors after distinguished playing careers. Alex died in 1976, aged 70.

To the uninitiated, close family associations with particular bands might suggest an element of nepotism, but this suggestion would be misplaced. So competitive is the brass band fraternity that bands cannot afford to carry passengers, however influential may be their connections. Harry Mortimer, discussing this question with the author, recalled that he and his brothers all wanted to join his father's band. 'But we had to earn our places. There was no favouritism just because we were the sons of the conductor,' he said.

These strong family connections which so frequently characterize the brass band scene are by no means merely historic: they are part of a continuing pattern. But no longer is it confined to male members of families. The growing emphasis on brass instrument instruction in schools is of significance for their is greater participation by girls and young women, a development which has also encouraged many boys to take up brass. The impact of female participation in the modern brass band movement is a substantial one. One of the younger bands, Kilmarnock Concert Brass, for example, which was formed in 1970 and in 1978 became the

Scottish champions, is unique in having 17 girls, including three sets of sisters, among its complement of 27.

The military musicians, whose musical prowess was a spur to the emulative instinct of musically inclined workers, were professionals. Other professional musicians in the commercial area were also an influence in the spread of music to the masses and to the impetus that was increasing among amateur bands. The circus was a popular entertainment and had its own musical accompaniment, although sometimes local bands were called upon to supply the music that added its own drama to that of the artists. Along with the Distin family the other most significant professional performer to influence the spread of music was a Frenchman, Louis Antoine Jullien, who came to England in 1839 and became one of the most controversial figures on the contemporary musical scene. To many he was regarded as a charlatan, but he claimed with some justification that it was he who first taught the masses what was best in music through the ingenious way he arranged his programmes, offering light and fluffy items as bait for the more serious content he included. His dynamic style of conducting and the introduction of effects to accompany the music – today they would be called gimmicks – were deliberately designed to capture and retain the attention of his audience. Apart from his London appearance Jullien made frequent provincial tours, and the performances of his soloists – Keonig on the cornet, Vivier on French horn and Prospère on the ophicleide, together with other talented instrumentalists – were admired as much for their talent as Jullien was applauded for his histrionics.

Jullien's showmanship would no doubt have appealed strongly to Enderby Jackson, himself a showman at heart as some of his later theatrical and commercial ventures proved, but Jackson was in no doubt about the contribution of the Jullien era to brass bands. 'The good effected by M. Jullien can never be over-estimated: unparalleled success always attended his Yorkshire and Lancashire tours. The "Jullien" concerts proved in the north the opening of a new era in advance of general musical art. Never before had such perfection been held up to our homely toilers as models for their guidance and imitative power,' he wrote. Jackson became positively ecstatic in his praise: 'New readings of works supposed well known, new forms of phrasing, new colourings of extremes in light and shade; peculiar rendering of uncommon harmonies and beautiful clear rendering of novel contrapuntal devices, rendered by the very highest procurable artists on their respective instruments. . . . These all proved sources of wonder and emulation to our music loving workmen and educational to our local professors and band teachers.' Brilliant showman he may have been, but other musical experts have praised Jullien's wide knowledge of the musical repertoire and his contribution to English music by, among other things, urging improved standards of performance. Jullien's career came to an early conclusion with his death at 49.

Hanwell Town Prize Band – a forerunner of the present Roneo-Vickers Band.

The stimulus had been provided from a number of sources. In village, town, workshop and colliery, men got together to form bands. By now the impetus had become nationwide, although the north of England was always to exercise a superiority in this form of music over other areas of the country. The movement grew into a large but nevertheless close community, reaching its golden era in the last 20 years of the nineteenth century. But its growth was in isolation from the rest of the musical scene. Whenever musicians from the wider musical sphere deigned to cast a glance in the direction of brass bands, they did so with some disbelief. Grove's *Dictionary of Music and Musicians* eventually gave brass bands a mention and the *Musical Times* occasionally commented on brass band events. Within the movement, however, there was scope for its own publications devoted to recording its many activities: *Brass Band News* which came into existence in 1881 through Wright & Round, the music publishers, and *The British Bandsman* which Samuel Cope inaugurated in 1887.

'There has always been a prejudice against brass bands,' Ernest Round wrote in his first editorial, in which he went on to castigate musical connoisseurs for forming their unfriendly opinions about brass bands from hearing indifferent, badly trained bands belching out commonplace quick marches in the street. 'To form a correct judgement one must hear a brass band contest', he advised. And there were plenty of these to choose from, varying from small band competitions to contests at trade exhibitions and, for the cream of brass bands, the British Open where all the crack bands performed each year.

By the latter years of the century economic progress had made life easier for the majority of the population and working class shoppers were able to purchase minor luxuries from the growing number of large departmental stores then coming into existence. Among them, especially in northern districts, were those run by the Co-operative movement which came to have close associations with the brass band movement. These are still preserved through the bands, such as those from the Manchester and Glasgow areas, sponsored by the Co-operative movement. The movement had been initiated in 1884 in Rochdale when a group of weavers invested £1 each to provide themselves with cheaper food. The example of the Rochdale Pioneers, as they came to be known, was followed elsewhere in towns in the north. Co-operative wholesale societies were set up to provide goods for the retail stores from their own factories: the C.W.S. Manchester Band was originally the Tobacco Factory Band. The movement's activities eventually extended beyond mere trading; they became involved in adult education and subsequently in politics.

The growth of bands included not only works-sponsored ensembles, although these were the biggest source: some had a purely political flavour like the Primrose bands which, it was noted in 1887, were springing up – bands associated with a Conservative Party group known as the Primrose League.

The actual number of bands in existence at this time is anybody's guess – and some fairly wild estimates have been made. They were said, somewhat incredibly, to be multiplying daily. The editor of *Brass Band News* claimed there were 40,000 amateur bands in the United Kingdom and numbers were rapidly increasing. This high figure was undoubtedly over-estimated. But whatever the true figure, brass bands were obviously flourishing as never before or since for that matter, and it was generally accepted that the main factor in this advance was the contest, which encouraged bandsmen to improve their musicianship and their standards of performance. 8,000 spectators and 35 contesting bands attended the Belle Vue contest in 1888 and a total of 222 contests throughout Britain in 1895 were typical statistics of the period. Brass bands had become not just a pastime but part of the pattern of life for a large section of the working community.

Chapter Two

The contest—a 'musical prize fight'

Apart from ardent Wagnerians dutifully listening to *The Ring* in its entirety, where would you find more than 6,000 music lovers risking incipient piles through sitting on hard seats for seven hours, fervently listening to the same piece of music performed 22 or more times in succession? It does happen every year at Belle Vue in Manchester and at the Royal Albert Hall in London, now the two main centres for brass band contests – the British Open in September and the National Championships in October. It also happens on a smaller scale at countless other contests throughout the country. The scenes stand comparison with Wembley on Cup Final day, but without the accompanying hooliganism and vandalism now associated with football.

The extraordinary fervour of brass band fanatics has to be seen to be believed. Tickets have invariably been sold months in advance and on the day coaches bringing bands and supporters converge on the two cities in turn, disgorging their cargoes of players, instruments and followers to fill the huge halls to capacity. On arrival, the first priority is to obtain a copy of the score of the test-piece; this is often more important than the programme. Enthusiasts will recognize the band that is playing; it is important to follow its interpretation of the finer points of the music.

The purists will follow their score intently, detecting the slightest deviation or defect in the performance of a particular player, often calling further attention to these lapses by the nodding of heads or discernible gasps. In between performances by succeeding bands, their showing is discussed in strong northern accents that display innate musical knowledge. The audiences are mixed in

*'A musical prize fight' was the title of an article describing a village brass band contest at Lofthouse in Yorkshire which appeared in *All the Year Round*, a periodical edited by Charles Dickens.

their content and often include entire families with young people showing as much enthusiasm as veteran musicians. Belle Vue, once the family playground of the north, provided in the heyday of the brass band a complete day of entertainment. While father listened to the bands, the greatest collection of top bands you are likely to find, mother and children could find acres of other amusement. Now, however, the zoological gardens are no more and other attractions have disappeared. The area now has a tarnished aspect with bingo and the raucous music of the nearby funfair contrasting incongruously with the fine performances of the musicians inside the contest hall. A noted brass band conductor of the 1930s, Fred Mortimer, objected to the noisy competition of the funfair; by a strange irony the championships there are now promoted by his eldest son, Harry Mortimer.

The enthusiasm of brass band supporters is unwavering and often hereditary, passed on through several generations dating back more than a century. Belle Vue has been the venue of the British Open Championship for more than 125 years: the National, for which the contestants in the various grades have evolved through a series of regional qualifying rounds, have been held in London for the past 80 years. And during the whole of that time the support and enthusiasm has been consistent and today is as fervent as it has ever been.

There are retired and venerable old players who look back nostalgically to what they would regard as the good old days of contesting, openly criticising some of the aspects of modern contests which they find unacceptable. Many, for instance, bemoan the comparatively recent introduction of percussion into brass bands. They are prepared to tolerate it in concert work but think it should be excluded from the serious business of contests. (There are, on the other hand, some enthusiasts who think bands without percussion should be excluded.)

The trophies, known among bandsmen as 'the pots', stand prominently displayed. At the National Championships, the silver trophy each band seeks to acquire, dented from an old mishap when unsuccessful bandsmen took exception to the verdict of the judges, stands on a pedestal like the familiar bust of Sir Henry Wood surveying the scene in the same hall at the annual Proms. The day here always concludes with a magnificent evening concert by massed bands, usually with a noted orchestral conductor on the rostrum, at which enthusiasts can enjoy the performance of combinations of the most talented and dedicated amateur musicians in the country.

Percussion instruments were only allowed in contests as recently as 1973.

The benefits of contesting have been debated since competitions were first held. Nowadays, some of the top bands confine their contesting to the two main events only. It is argued that the preparation necessary for a test-piece in a contest takes up too much rehearsal time and that more benefit accrues to the band movement through public concerts. The title of 'champion band' means less than the title implies when the reality of the situation is that, as happened in the 1979 British Open Championship, the winning band was only one point ahead of its nearest rival and only five points separated the six prize-winners. It certainly says something for the high quality of the performances.

There can be no denying, however, that contesting has provided the great strength of the brass band movement from its earliest days. There has always been intense but friendly rivalry among bands and bandsmen and competition between them dates back to the movement's infancy when challenges were thrown down and readily accepted wherever bandsmen met.

Political elections were much livelier events in the last century than the hustings of today and the earliest challenges came when bands were recruited by opposing parties or candidates to help enliven the elections or to lead processions on election day. These challenges were usually of a purely musical and non-political nature; the one who paid the highest fee was often of more importance.

There are references to contests as early as 1818, though the earliest were small and unofficial. One of these took place in 1821 at a procession on the occasion of the coronation of George IV in which several bands, including Besses o' th' Barn, were participating. To pass the time while they waited for the large procession to be martialled, a subscription list was spontaneously organized to award a prize to the band which best played a piece of music of its own selection. Besses Band won with, appropriately enough, its rendering of the National Anthem, a wise choice in view of the occasion.

During the 1830s when the change to full brass bands was gaining impetus, a new band was formed at Hull with the financial help of local gentry whose generous donations to the creation of a band worthy of the city and the East Riding of Yorkshire enabled the purchase of first-class instruments. What is perhaps of greater significance, though, is the fact that among the players in the trumpet section was a nine-year-old boy who, in later years, was to become the most distinguished brass band entrepreneur. His name was Enderby Jackson, whose lasting contribution to the brass band movement will be referred to later.

Among the East Riding gentry who gave encouragement was Sir Clifford Constable, who was in the enviable position of employing his own bandmaster at his stately home at Burton Constable Hall. The bandmaster, George Leng, had a comprehensive musical ability extending to both brass and string instruments. Sir Clifford's sister-in-law, Lady Chichester, had also been impressed by both the quality of the numerous bands then being formed in the country and the band contests she had seen while holidaying in the south of France, a country that was then ahead of Britain when it came to musical competition. Sir Clifford was persuaded into including, with the help of Leng's organization, a contest between rival bands as part of a massive fête in the grounds of the Hall in 1845. Five bands participated. Particular conditions were laid down for the contest: there were to be no drums, in case they disguised weaknesses or obscured some of the finer musical points, and the number of players in each band was limited to 12, a restriction which led to some borrowing of players. This was a factor which was to become a controversial issue in future contests after it became established procedure to produce groupings of the most talented players.

It was during the Great Exhibition of 1851, in which many

brass bands took part, that the first moves were made to inaug-
urate regular contests. The nine-year-old trumpeter in the Hull
Band of 1836 was now an established and ambitious musician
who saw a potentially great future for brass bands. At the Exhibition, Jackson met two other brass band musicians of matching
enthusiasm, James A. Melling of Stalybridge, and Tallis Trimnell
of Chesterfield – 'both young musicians full of ardent zeal in
spreading the love of music broadly among the teeming population of operatives and miners surrounding their central districts'.
Jackson discussed with them the progress of amateur brass bands
in Yorkshire and of contests at fêtes and other events which had
followed the first Burton Constable contest six years earlier. This
progress was discussed in the light of the encouragement of special
excursions – originated by Thomas Cook some years earlier – by
the expanding railway companies, and it was agreed that the
railway companies' co-operation should be sought in transporting
bands at special rates to a central point where they could compete
against each other under a carefully considered set of rules for
their conduct.

The changeover to wholly brass bands had not yet been fully
accomplished by this time. The first result of the discussions was
a contest the following year for drum and fife bands. It was a
successful experiment. Belle Vue, of course, being a commercial
enterprise was anxious to fill its programme with a wide range of
events. James Melling and the Belle Vue manager, John Jennison,
saw the potential and, encouraged by the success of their experiments, organized the first brass band contest there the following
year, 1853. It became an annual event and continues to this day
with all the vitality, enthusiasm and competitiveness of those early
contests. It has made Belle Vue synonymous with brass bands.
Special contest compositions are now a regular feature of contests.
And Belle Vue can claim another 'first' in this respect: Melling
was the composer in 1855 of the first test-piece, an overture
entitled *Orynthia*. It was more than half a century before the
practice caught on.

It is recorded that Enderby Jackson's idea of staging a brass
band contest first came to him during race week at Doncaster in
the early 1850s. Jackson at that time was playing in a touring
orchestra. He described later how the 'revelation' came to him.
After the races he was chatting in the bandroom when another
member of the orchestra remarked that while prizes were given
to horses at races and to cattle and pigs at agricultural shows for
their excellence, nobody gave prizes to musicians to stimulate

them to excel. 'These words sank deep into my heart', he wrote later in his customary dramatic style. 'I saw the excitement produced. Was it entirely to see the horses run that people cared about? No, thought I. It is the rivalry and if this rivalry could be instituted amongst workmen with music instead of horses my work would be inaugurated.'

Enderby Jackson meanwhile was gaining a considerable reputation as a promoter of brass band contests, his field of operations covering a wider geographical radius over the northern countries. His first big contest took place in his native Hull in 1856, at which he demonstrated his confidence in publicity and public relations as a necessary and successful adjunct to organizing ability in these matters. Six months before the event he set out on a public relations crusade to towns in the manufacturing and industrial regions of the north, meeting band officials where bands already existed and, where they did not, encouraging the setting up of new bands and supporters clubs to accompany them to the contest, taking advantage of the excursion trains he was organizing with the railway companies. He returned to Hull well satisfied with the response and the promises he had received over the raising of bands. One of his suggestions to advertise the contest was that bands should parade locally. On the day, 21 bands took part, all of them marching from the station to the contest in the Zoological Gardens.

The competitive element was becoming an essential feature of the movement and Jackson began to build up his reputation as a promoter. He was in great demand, a peripatetic promoter organizing contests in York, Sheffield, Chesterfield, Birmingham and other cities. Apart from those at Belle Vue or those which bore the Jackson stamp on them, there was an increasing number of smaller contests. The same bands appeared at almost all the contests, jostling for the first three positions: one band in 1859 entered for at least six contests in different centres.

The rewards were tremendous in both esteem and money. Bands could net what were then large sums in prize money. Amounts of £1,500 amassed over a period of several years were not unusual and, when used to furnish the band with better instruments or to provide them with their own practice room, the successes could be even better. In the early days of contesting, however, the rewards were sometimes of a more tangible kind, if less musically useful. Meat often appeared among the trophies, particularly in contests held in rural parts of Lancashire, and many a band returned triumphantly to its home town bearing the carcase of a sheep or, occasionally, trying to cope with the antics of a live animal acquired as part of the prize-winning pay-off.

As prize money began to increase along with the opportunities for bands to compete for these financial rewards, examples of sophistry became increasingly apparent and did nothing to enhance the reputation of brass bands in the wider musical sphere. Instruments had to be carefully guarded to prevent any deliberate tampering with them before a contest. Judges were often accused of favouritism; results were not always received in a sportsmanlike manner. Bands often deliberately arrived late to avoid having to play first. On one occasion at a contest in Leicester the unfortunate adjudicator was greeted with derisive shouts when a band, which some enthusiasts considered to be inferior to their own, was announced as the winner. The judge was chased across the field by officials and irate performers and spectators. To avoid the consequence of capture, he pleaded he had made a mistake, and was taken back to the stage to announce a new winner which on this occasion satisfied the hostile audience.

Fred Mortimer, in a newspaper interview, once compared the modern, efficiently organized contests with strict enforcement of rules, high level of sportsmanship and deportment shown by competitors – all of which brought acknowledged prestige to the movement – with some of the conditions when he was a youth. Rough houses were not unusual, with those bandsmen not awarded prizes creating scenes and threatening the judges. Local rivalries were really bitter. 'I was once stoned off the concert platform,' he recalled. Contests were held in the open air in rough and ready conditions. Bandsmen were in mufti, usually playing in a circle round the conductor with their jackets off. It was not unknown for other bands to break into test performances with a noisy accompaniment of their own if the performing band had broken a rule and got away with it. The sweeping changes Fred Mortimer saw in his lifetime in brass bands transformed the movement from an unco-ordinated and often disparaged movement into a vital cultural force. But at the time disorderly behaviour only contributed to the isolation of the movement by the wider musical fraternity. The displays of Cup Final fever were not conducive to the movement's wider acceptance.

The main strength of the brass band movement at this time was among mill operatives in Lancashire and Yorkshire, a fact which is evident from the predominance of entries of works bands at the growing number of contests then being organized. The disorderly elements among the ranks were more than matched by the steadfast support and loyalty of serious-minded working people, and the influential leadership of men like Enderby Jackson who was able to channel the enthusiasm of a group of very independently-minded people in directions that built a solid base for the movement.

From Lancashire and Yorkshire the message was spreading northwards to Scotland and southwards to the Midlands and beyond. The movement was being almost revolutionized by the advent of contests. They provided a great incentive to improve standards of playing and behaviour, both of which were entirely beneficial to the movement as a whole, which was at serious risk of reaping what could have been a thoroughly disreputable name through the disorderly conduct and corrupt practices at some of the small contests.

Enderby Jackson was called on to organize contests on a fairly large scale elsewhere. After the contest held at Hull in 1856, which was attended by 12,000 people, there followed one at Sheffield two years later for which he composed a set of Yorkshire waltzes as the test-piece. The interest these contests aroused was reflected in the increasing number of bands being formed. One seemed to lead to the other. Jackson later recalled that within a few years almost every village and group of mills in Lancashire and Yorkshire east and west of the Pennines owned its own band. 'It mattered not to them how the bands were constituted or what classification of instruments was in use; each man made his own choice and the teacher found music suitably arranged for their proficiency. If these things were cleverly managed, music was the result: and music was the love and pride of these people and their ever-abiding pastime.'

It was inevitable with the profusion of bands southwards that the prospect of a London contest would arise. Joseph Paxton's great glass construction that had housed the 1851 Exhibition had been moved and rebuilt at Sydenham in South London where its improved acoustics were making it a popular venue for musical events. Jackson negotiated with the managers for a brass band contest, the first of four annual events, to be held there in 1860. At the same time he obtained concessionary fares from the railway companies which enabled, for example, bandsmen and their families to travel between Leeds and London for only 4s. 6d. (approximately 45p). The contest was spread over two days with 75 bands entered for the first day and 98 for the second. Black Dyke Mills was placed first and, therefore, excluded from the second day's contest, which was won by a Welsh band, Cyfartha. Over the two days the contest attracted an audience of 27,000 people. It included concerts by massed bands of 1,390 players, conducted by Enderby Jackson, playing patriotic items such as *Rule Britannia* and the National Anthem, Mendelssohn's *Wedding March* and the Hallelujah Chorus with what a reporter from *The Times* described as an astounding effect, 'the host of players exerting themselves with a zeal and unanimity worthy of unqualified praise'.

This first contest, said the report, went off with great spirit and presented features of uncommon interest. In the morning 44 bands appeared before the judges, playing on six specially erected platforms in various parts of the huge building. Then, in the afternoon, they joined together for the concert. The effect of the combined legions of 'blowers' was tremendous. They were accompanied by the organ which, the writer said, on less exceptional occasions tended to drown everything else but was now scarcely audible amid this 'brass tempest'. Nothing less than Henry Distin's 'monster gong drum', the thunder of which required the united efforts of two men, could prevail against it. Distin's drum was a remarkable instrument that had been introduced to the musical public three years earlier. Seven feet in diameter, its skin was reputed to be the largest buffalo hide ever imported, which had been reduced by machinery from its original quarter-inch thickness. The rim of the drum consisted of 30 dovetailed pieces. It was the *Wedding March* and the National Anthem which pleased the audience most and encores were given for both items.

The whole concert was conducted with 'wonderful vigour and precision' by Enderby Jackson who, the writer said, had exerted himself in forwarding the brass band movement among the mechanics, artisans, petty tradesmen, manufacturers and labourers of northern and midland counties with energy and unremitting zeal. After this colossal display the 12 bands selected by the judges as the most worthy to contend for the prizes exhibited their strength and capabilities. There was no disagreement here with the judges: no chasing them through the Crystal Palace Park. 'Taking into consideration the extreme delicacy of their task, it is more than probable that the decision come to by the judges will be submitted to with a very general good taste', he wrote.

The Times reporter was back at Crystal Palace the next day among the even larger attendance of 22,000 – a number which he thought helped to give vigour and spirit to the proceedings. The preliminary trials were taken as before, then the whole force again exhibited its strength in the same selected programme. This time, though, the effect was more astounding, with three encores for *Rule Britannia*, the *Wedding March* and the National Anthem, all of which were executed with 'surprising brilliancy and precision'. Mr Bowley, general manager of Crystal Palace, presented the prizes and expressed his belief in the good results that must accrue from the movement. 'For a first experiment of this kind the success was quite extraordinary', was the verdict of the man from *The Times*.

The Crystal Palace contest did not, however, at that time become an annual event such as that as Belle Vue. The fourth meeting in the Crystal Palace series over, Jackson extended his activities as an impresario over a wider sphere, organizing tours abroad for concert companies, drama groups and orchestras. He unfortunately suffered ill-health, a factor which prevented him from becoming concert manager of Australia's Melbourne Opera House, and his managerial activities were interspersed with more restful periods in which he indulged in his hobbies and writing at his home in Scarborough. There he died in 1903 at the age of 77 in the happy knowlege that, by encouraging healthy competition between brass bands in a properly organized form, he had laid solid foundations for what was to become the strong national movement of brass bands in British music today.

The fact that a Welsh band was among the prizewinners at Crystal Palace in 1860 and a London Volunteer Band successfully entered the 'holy land' of Belle Vue the following year illustrate the extent to which brass bands were becoming a national movement. Cyfartha, the winning band at Crystal Palace, was the outstanding Welsh band of the period, but it consisted of English players from across the border. Its success, however, did give impetus to Welsh interest which had gained momentum by the 1880s when large-scale contests lured to the Principality some of the leading bands in the north of England. The importance of brass bands in the cultural life of Wales was quickly realized by eisteddfod organizers who began to include sections for brass bands in their programmes. Since then, brass band competitions have become enshrined – and still are – in these unique annual cultural gatherings.

Meanwhile, in Scotland it was the Volunteer Movement from which contesting derived, with the first Scottish contests being promoted during the 1860s by H.D. Douglas, a Glasgow instrument-maker. These were later extended in their appeal as more civilian brass bands were formed. The first English bands to cross the border for competitions did so in 1877 at a contest in Edinburgh, which was a trendsetter in this respect since, in the following decade, a number of the leading British bands were appearing in Scottish contests. International exhibitions in Edinburgh in 1886 and in Glasgow two years later provided additional occasions for large scale contests, with up to 20 English bands taking part in the open contest. It was not until after the turn of the century, in 1904, that Musselburgh and Fishbarrow Trades Band became the first Scottish band to take back a prize from England, having won a band contest at Newcastle.

Hundreds of smaller contests were being organized, but the Belle Vue Championship reigned unchallenged for almost half a century as the principal competition. As more bands were formed more entries were received, until the organizers were becoming overwhelmed. The average number of entries at Belle Vue was 40, but time allowed for the acceptance of only half that number. In 1886 the contest had to be divided to meet the demand into two graded sections with supplementary contests being held in July. No band which had won a prize at the September contests in the previous four years could enter, a restriction which gave a better chance to lesser bands: it was also a qualifying competition for the September contests.

The large-scale and well-organized contests were now big business, for both Belle Vue and for the railway companies, who laid on as many as 50 excursion trains to bring up to 10,000 supporters. Throughout the country it was estimated there were altogether about 240 contests of varying sizes and quality by 1896. They created vast opportunities for some bands to indulge in 'pot hunting' – the acquisition of cups – in the quest for which some of them would indulge in almost any practice of subterfuge in order to win. One unfair practice was that of borrowed players: bands often paid for the services of a leading player from another band to improve their performance, particularly in a weak section. It was a practice common among bands for many years and, because of its wide use, resulted in strong reactions from supporters until it was ultimately eradicated by contest organizers imposing more rigorous restrictions on players. Nowadays, all players have to be registered and their credentials can be checked through the central registry.

The desire to have the best available players may have derived from a 'pot hunting' instinct, but it could also be said to show a desire to have the best performers for the sake of the music. Other factors contributed to a higher standard of performance, the most notable being that the music available to brass bands was changing. Band trainers, some of whom were very distinguished musicians such as Charles Godfrey, bandmaster of the Royal Horse Guards, were attempting to break away from the familiar marches and music hall song arrangements by arranging operatic selections. These had the dual effect of presenting a challenge to the players while introducing higher quality music to areas which might not otherwise have heard them. The items were usually arranged as contest test-pieces but rapidly came to form part of the brass band concert repertoire.

Another factor which contributed to the higher standards of brass band music was the 'own choice' contest, which formed nearly half the total number of contests then being held throughout the country. By this method, a band selected its own test-piece and worked hard at its performance and interpretation through hours of rehearsal. One criticism of 'own choice' music was that certain pieces of music came to be associated with particular bands and there was concern that judges could often identify a band by the piece it played. Many of the works were lengthy and ambitious, bearing in mind they were being performed by amateur musicians who were working men first and musicians second. They included arrangements of excerpts from such magnificent works as Wagner's *Tristan and Isolde* and *Die Valkyrie*, items which required up to half-an-hour for their performance. For some supporters they were too long and over-ambitious. In the years up to the First World War such items appeared prominently in the programmes of provincial concerts and were still performed for many years to come. But gradually they were being replaced by original compositions for the brass band. Some original music was being written around this time, but there was still a deep divide between brass bands and the rest of the musical world and some years were to elapse before original works were produced from the pens of distinguished composers writing purely for the brass band.

Twenty years after that meeting during the 1851 Exhibition from which emanated the first major contests at Belle Vue, John Henry Iles, a man destined to play an equally important role in contesting and encouraging the brass band movement, was born in Bristol. Iles displayed an interest in music at an early age, which was encouraged during the six years he was a pupil at Ashville College in Harrogate: he was also gifted with a flair for organizing, both qualities from which the brass band movement was to benefit in large measure. He studied solo singing, with Clara Butt as a fellow pupil, and when he went into business it was almost inevitable that he would find some way of combining his musical interests with his plans for a successful business career. He did it by taking over the control of a number of musical periodicals including *The Organist and Choirmaster*. While Enderby Jackson was the nineteenth-century catalyst of the brass band movement, John Henry Iles was the central figure around which the movement revolved during the first half of the twentieth century, but the spark that ignited this dynamic man came in the closing stages of the previous century.

Iles was in Manchester on business - attempting to buy Belle Vue it is said – and with time to spare was persuaded to attend the Belle Vue contest of 1898. He was astonished to learn that such skilled performers were amateur musicians from a working-class background that was often, to say the least, grim and poverty stricken. He went to the contest reluctantly but came away a completely converted enthusiast for the cause: he believed the movement should be more widely known and appreciated and vowed he would use his increasing influence on behalf of these talented musicians. Iles, years later, recalled that experience in a letter to *The Times*. 'When I first heard our then champion bands at Belle Vue in 1898 I made a vow that I would do my best to make the country sing with appreciation of the remarkable talent among our workers', he wrote. 'Like most people of those days to me the very name of brass could only mean noise and discord, and I had the musical surprise of my life when I heard them playing as if for their lives in the Belle Vue championship. It took me some time to realize that I was listening to amateurs and working men.' He first extended his publishing interests by buying the brass band musicians' 'trade paper', *The British Bandsman*, and the music publishing firm of R. Smith & Co Ltd, both of which are still very much in business. He also became involved with the then struggling London and Home Counties Brass Band Association, whose president, Sam Cope, had conceived the idea of starting the magazine in 1887 to try to improve the position of brass bandsmen in the musical world.

Iles hit on the idea of bringing the great northern championship bands to London for a concert in the Royal Albert Hall. In the flamboyant style by which he was to become known, he aimed high in his organization of the concert, enlisting the help of another flamboyant man and press baron, Lord Northcliffe, whose *Daily Mail* Kipling Fund for the relatives of soldiers fighting in the Boer War was to benefit from the proceeds. It became known as the 'Absent-Minded Beggar' Concert, through Rudyard

Kipling's poem of that title which, in a musical setting by Sir Arthur Sullivan, of which Iles owned the rights, was being played throughout the country by brass and military bands.

Sir Arthur Sullivan had said he would never conduct another rendering of the famous composition and had resisted various requests to do so, but he had not reckoned with the persuasiveness of J. Henry Iles. Lord Northcliffe had issued a challenge to Iles which had been readily accepted. Northcliffe had tried unsuccessfully, despite the offer of attractive financial rewards, to get Sullivan to conduct his composition again. He told Iles that if he succeeded in getting Sullivan to conduct the march he would sponsor Iles's plan to run a great concert of brass bands at the Royal Albert Hall. Northcliffe never thought he would succeed. His first approach was to Sir Arthur's secretary, Wilfred Bendall, who told him the idea was utterly useless. But Iles persisted and eventually Sir Arthur agreed to see him, if only to satisfy his curiosity about this persistent man. Within half-an-hour Iles had aroused Sullivan's enthusiasm: not only had he agreed to conduct the massed bands but they had managed to agree the entire programme and selected the soloists.

A dense fog descended on London on the night of the concert, 20 January, 1900, but it failed to deter the 10,000 ticket holders (half as many again were turned away) from a glittering occasion. Eleven brass bands took part, representing the main banding centres: Black Dyke Mills, Besses o' th' Barn, Wyke Temperance, Hartlepool Operatic, Hucknall Temperance, Kettering Rifles, St Albans City, Clydebank, Ballymacarriff, Nantille Vale and Arael Griffin. Iles's former fellow pupil, Clara Butt, was among the soloists.

The concert was a financial success for the relatives of the Boer War soldiers, but it was also of great significance to the future of the brass band movement. J. H. Elliot in *The Brass Band Movement* recalls Iles narrating to him how he stood at Sullivan's side on the platform and how the composer was deeply moved and vastly impressed by the achievements of the bands, which had played separately as well as in massed concert. He turned to Iles and enquired: 'What can be done for these fellows?'

Iles's fertile mind was not slow to find an answer. Like Enderby Jackson 40 years earlier, Iles also cherished the idea of an annual brass band festival in London. Sir Arthur Sullivan was then one of the directors of Crystal Palace and plans were immediately set in motion. The Thousand Guinea Trophy, which had originally been provided by the Crystal Palace authorities for competition at the choral festivals at the Palace, had been stored in the vaults since their discontinuance some years earlier; it was dusted and cleaned and, at Sullivan's insistence, offered as the main prize for the competing bands.

Iles was undeterred by the discouragement he received from others, remembering the lack of success of Jackson's earlier attempts to initiate an annual festival in London and he proceeded with his plans. His idea was to create a 'stepping stone' competition, with a progressive series of graded concerts that would enable bands of varying ability to compete at their respective levels.

His ideas came to fruition and the first National Band Festival was held later that year on 27 July, 1900. Twenty-nine bands took part in three grades: many of the best-known bands were there including Besses o' th' Barn, Black Dyke Mills, Wingate Temperance and Irwell Springs. The test-piece in the main section was, appropriately enough, a selection from Sullivan's operas.

The Times reported the occasion, although the brief report was tucked away in small type at the bottom of a page of mainly foreign news snippets, an indication perhaps that the brass band movement, although having the Sullivan seal of approval, still had a long way to go to get wider acceptance. The competition attracted an enormous crowd, though, and the reporter stressed the object: to spread the cult of brass band music in the south of England.

There was one brief incident during the competition which, while perhaps illustrating the intense feelings that could be aroused, also contributed no doubt to the reluctance of the musical establishment to accept brass bands on equal terms. 'The festival was entirely successful except for one incident which was indeed most regrettable. Immediately after the announcement of the names of the prize-winners several of the bands, whose names are best left unmentioned, left the Palace disappointed at not winning the first prize,' reported *The Times*, with its customary discretion. 'Such conduct is unsportsmanlike in the extreme and if this is to be the result of competitions music would be better without them,' it added tartly. The *British Bandsman* also remonstrated with the offending bandsmen. 'We can understand the great disappointment of some of the crack bands in finding themselves out of the prizes after giving fine performances, but they should remember that it does not always follow that the best band wins. It is the best performance of the day in the opinion of the judges that decides the prize list.'

The following year there was a disappointing entry of only 27 bands and in 1902 Iles announced that area contests would be held which would result in invitations to take part in the National Championships. It was a decision that proved to be unpopular in some areas and several of the proposed area contests had to be abandoned. 'Second class bands have been only too ready to dispute the right of such combinations as Besses, Dyke, Wyke, etc., to consider themselves in a class by themselves or at any rate to be chosen upon their undoubtedly great reputations. Upon what else can the position of these bands be gauged?' asked the *British Bandsman*. 'In giving such a question a fair amount of consideration, one could only conclude that a contest arranged on strict lines in every sense of the word was the only possible means of settling the matter in a way fair to all. Let those bands who consider themselves as good as the great "cracks" already referred to prove their opinions in honest fight and then who shall say nay?' The editorial went on to explain that the arrangements had been introduced with the sole object of giving a chance to rising and progressive bands to prove their mettle and win by a fair fight the right to be considered among the 'crack' bands. 'If young bands have no ambition and enterprise, how can they expect to rival those who have made their names famous in brass band history?' Despite criticism of the new arrangements there were nearly 100 entries on the day and a satisfactory contest ensued.

The brass band movement could truly be described as entering a new era as the twentieth century approached. Devotees were no longer content with passive observance and many felt an impulse to take a more active part. The resulting upsurge in the number of bandsmen over the country was evidence that Iles's intention to increase brass band awareness was succeeding. In between organizing the annual contents, he was increasingly extending his role of impresario, arranging tours by Besses o' th' Barn Band in this country and abroad, culminating in a world tour in 1906/7, although Black Dyke Mills Band beat them to New York by a mere month. He was also responsible for an interchange of bands, bringing groups from other countries to tour Britain. Meanwhile, the annual festival was becoming firmly established. The disappointing response in the second year was short-lived; interest grew along with the number of entrants each year. From 90 bands in 1902, there were 117 the following year; by 1908 there were five grades and in 1910 over 200 bands entered, of which only 160 could be accepted.

Callender's Cable Works Band from Belvedere, Kent, pictured in 1925. It was augmented by several players from St Hilda's Band when that band turned professional in 1927. Callender's was at one time probably the leading southern band and presented a serious challenge to the north country bands.

Contest regulations were now being rigorously enforced, and because of some of the pecularities of the contest arrangements, band contests stood apart from other musical competitions. One of the eccentricities was the rigid control of the adjudicators, which was not exercised in other areas of competitive music. The first action of contest organizers was to elect by ballot a supervisory committee which then installed the judges in a tent or box-like room with a policeman on duty at the entrance with instructions that no person must be permitted to communicate with them. How different this was from other musical events can be illustrated from the author's own experience as a young journalist reporting a musical festival in Yorkshire some years ago at which he was permitted to sit alongside Dr Herbert Howells while he was judging a solo singing class. The experience of hearing 50 young singers separately rendering *Nymphs and Shepherds* throughout an entire morning left the author eternally sympathetic towards all music festival judges.

The order of play is drawn by representatives of each band, and, hidden away from sight as they are in their judging box, the adjudicators know the bands only by their number. The judging is by notes of the merits and demerits of each competing band and the judges' awards are arrived at by totalling the marks awarded for various aspects of the bands' performances. The supervisory committee release the judges from their solitary confinement and they then either announce the results themselves or hand them in writing to the official in charge to announce. The notes of the judges are usually made available later to the contestants who, hopefully, in future contests put right their mistakes.

While judges were now perhaps spared the dangers and indignities of early contest behaviour when an adverse decision was given, they nevertheless often had to endure uncomfortable conditions shut away in their box, untainted by outside distractions. In the early days of the Belle Vue contests the judges' box was an elevated loft-like construction lined with two thicknesses of heavy blanket spaced a foot apart. This double shield can have done little to help the acoustics. It had a deadening effect on the sound and one judge has recalled how bands seemed as a result to be playing at only half power. Later, lighter material was substituted for the blankets. There were often oversuspicious minds convinced that loopholes were being found to communicate to judges, or subterfuges to indicate which band was playing. On one occasion at Belle Vue a very capable adjudicator with a sense of humour invited an inspection committee to look under the table for possible loopholes. One member of a less humorous nature accepted – to find only the spectacle of three pairs of adjudicators' legs and an outsize chamber pot. On another occasion in the hushed seconds before one of the bands started to play, the conductor accidentally knocked over his music stand. The conductor of the following band thought he had detected a pre-arranged signal to the adjudicator and when his turn came, in order to forestall the arrangement, he deliberately kicked over his stand as he mounted the rostrum.

In more recent times a new type of box was devised for use in the Royal Albert Hall, where the National Championships have been held since 1945. It was, not surprisingly, christened 'the refrigerator', but with its improved lighting, noiseless air conditioning and ample desk room, adjudicators found it a vast improvement on the old boxes. Audibility was perfect and since it was erected in close proximity to the stage, few sounds – good or bad– failed to reach the adjudicators' ears. There are many enthusiasts who believe all these precautions are now no longer necessary: that they have merely become part of the brass band tradition and that in any case many bands have a playing style and sound of their own which makes them easily distinguishable to a practised ear. At the time of writing there are plans by the organizers to dispense with 'the box' at the 1980 National Championships*, an example which if successful will surely be followed by many other contest organizers. Judges at an annual contest at Morecambe, started in 1948, have always been in the open.

Another aspect of band contests which is alien to other musical competitions is the sporting element. Large sums of money are reported to have changed hands, particularly in the colliery districts of South Wales and Durham, through widespread wagering on the result of a competition.

The next major step forward in contesting, which was also to have an important impact on the movement generally, was yet another of the contributions of Henry Iles. Only a small amount of music available had been especially composed for brass bands: their repertoire in the main still consisted of marches, arrangements of operatic selections and popular songs. While the musical world continued largely to ignore what was developing into a strong force in national musical life, there were passing references and criticisms in some sections of the musical press to this deficiency. These chided the movement over the available music, especially some of the test-pieces which were mosaics of various musical bits and pieces. It was still associated strongly with outdoor music with an appropriate repertoire. Iles saw an opportunity here to lift up brass bands into a more acceptable position in the wider world of music. He sought to do so through commissioning special works from composers for use as championship test-pieces. The first was commissioned for the 1913 contest from Percy Fletcher, whose compositions were to become firm favourites with brass bandsmen and have been performed – and still are – by successive generations of bandsmen. He produced a tone poem entitled *Labour and Love*. The following year Cyril Jenkins wrote *Coriolanus* for the contest, but the war intervened – Crystal Palace was occupied throughout the war by the Admiralty – and it was 1920 before that work was performed as the national test-piece, although it had been played elsewhere at contests earlier in the same year.

Unlike the National, the contests at Belle Vue were maintained throughout the years of the war: Iles's policy of commissioning test-pieces was extended there when he became managing director of Belle Vue in 1925. The impact of distinguished composers

*In fact these plans did not materialise.

writing for the brass band will be discussed separately: suffice to say here that the movement received an impetus which propelled it considerably nearer the goal of general acceptance when composers of the calibre of Edward Elgar, Gustav Holst and John Ireland began composing for contests from 1928 onwards.

Crystal Palace remained the venue for the National Championship and festival until its destruction by fire in 1936. This was a disastrous loss since, like Belle Vue, in the north, Crystal Palace had become synonymous in the south of England with brass band music. Iles, on hearing the news, expressed the hope that the Palace would be re-built, but it never was. The following year the festival was moved north of the Thames to Alexandra Palace, a spacious edifice on the northern heights of London, noted at that time for its musical activities in the Great Hall. It was an appropriate choice but serious factors were at work on the international scene that were to prevent it becoming a permanent home for the National. The crisis in international affairs from 1938 onwards and the war that followed inevitably brought the abandonment of the competition for the duration. Bandsmen exchanged their colourful, gold-braided, Ruritanian uniforms for drab khaki. Despite wartime difficulties many of them kept up their playing in service bands – and others left at home fortunately kept the civilian bands in existence ready for peacetime.

With the end of the war there came important changes. Henry Iles, the predominant figure in the movement for nearly half a century, was now over 70 and anxious to ensure the long-term future of the championships. The venue was changed to the Royal Albert Hall and publicity people became involved in the organization of the events through the *Daily Herald*, which had been invited to assist in re-establishing the national festival. Otherwise the pattern for the first peacetime contest remained similar to the pre-war competitions. Throughout the summer of 1945 area contests had been held among invited bands, 17 of which ended up in the first National competition for six years after winning through. The ending of the war had inspired the music for the test-piece: Denis Wright's *Overture to an Epic Occasion*. Dr Malcolm Sargent deputized at short notice for Sir Adrian Boult as the principal conductor of the massed bands concert in the evening, at which five bands played that splendid brass band item *Finlandia*; and two new works, also inspired by the recent events, *Normandy* by Henry Gheel and a lively march entitled *Whitehall* by Frank Wright, were conducted by Harry Mortimer. It was exactly 100 years since the first official contest had taken place at Burton

Constable Hall, near Hull; the re-establishment of the contests and the atmosphere at the evening concert provided a suitable celebration. It also proved that the enthusiasm and fervour of the brass band movement was as great and responsive as it had ever been, despite the years of wartime interruption.

It was perhaps appropriate that of all the national newspapers it was the *Daily Herald*, with its own close associations with the working classes, that should take the contests under its wing. Jerome Chester, the newspaper's publicity director, had persuaded the Odhams Press management to take on the responsibilties. Henry Iles, with a sense of relief at the successful outcome of the discussions on sponsorship, wrote: '. . . a dream and desire I have had in view for many years has at last come into active being. Thanks to the broad and practical vision of the *Daily Herald* management, I am very confident nothing but complete success can result.'

The new management realized that, along with all the goodwill from the past, a new approach was called for to encourage every band in the belief that they all had an equal opportunity of competing in the National Championships. It was felt that the pre-war events, although enabling a good number of bands to compete in the various sections, nevertheless had an element of restriction and discrimination through the presentation. Expert promotion men were seconded to the planning. The result was the definition of eight geographical regions, with the formation of local committees in each comprised of qualified brass band enthusiasts to help in arranging area qualifying finals. The areas were defined as Scotland, North East (Durham and Northumberland), Northern (Yorkshire), Midland (Nottinghamshire, Warwickshire and Shropshire), North West (Lancashire, Cheshire, North Wales and Cumberland), London and Southern Counties, West of England and South and West Wales. There were four distinct sections in each of the eight area finals: championship, second, third and fourth sections. Bands gaining first or second places in each of the four sections were invited to take part in the national finals in London. Test-pieces were carefully chosen for the qualifying rounds, as they were for the national finals.

Another innovation introduced by the new sponsors was the national Brass Band Registry, set up to regularize and control the official playing members of individual brass bands. Its greatest achievement was the removal of some of the malpractices that had often marred competitions. The Registry has now become an

CAMELFORD TOWN BAND - 1913

The West Country too had its share of brass bands early this century – and it remains an area where they are popular. Here are two Cornish bands: *above* Camelford Town Band in 1913 and *below* Redruth Town Band, pictured in 1916.

REDRUTH TOWN BAND

integral part of contesting and there are more than 100,000 names and details of bandsmen recorded on its files.

There was inevitably some antagonism towards the new arrangements but some firm leading articles in Iles's own periodical, the *British Bandsman*, soon overcame the opposition and the future looked bright. And so it was for a couple of decades, thanks largely to the emergence of another dominant figure from the *Daily Herald* management team, Edwin Vaughan-Morris, who became the driving force in the organization of the championships throughout that period.

The *Daily Herald* management had undoubtedly been influenced in its decision to sponsor the championships by the potential new readership which so vast a movement presented. The newspaper devoted a weekly article to news and features about the popular movement. The cloth cap associations had not yet been divested, another factor which must have appealed to the management of the newspaper which, itself backed by the Trades Union Congress and perpetuating class divisions of earlier eras, was recognized as the organ of working-class readers. But brass bands were changing among their followers and this potential readership among bandsmen, did not materialize. Even if it had, it would have been no match for the intricacies of newspaper economics which resulted in the *Daily Herald* ceasing publication in 1964. The control of the championships passed to the Herald's sister paper, *The People*. But the upheaval had a deep effect on the movement and created a feeling of insecurity which had an almost immediate effect on the championships in 1965 when one in five bands withdrew from the area contests.

The People announced that they would be discontinued and that the National Registry and the National Brass Band Contesting Council, the co-ordinating body for the contests, would cease to exist. The national finals and festival concerts, which *The People* would continue to organize, were to consist of invited bands.

The future of the National Registry was quickly resolved. In December 1965 it was handed over to the management of Belle Vue, Manchester, who still maintain it with the support of brass band associations. Some areas, with independent-minded Yorkshire leading the way, decided to run their own regional contests. Yet another shock was in store. The International Publishing Corporation, which had bought out Odhams Press, had a retirement policy under which all senior members of the staff were compelled to retire at a specified age. Edwin Vaughan-Morris, who had then been responsible for organizing the championships for 20 years and had, in the words of *The British Bandsman* 'planned, built and worked like a tiger to bring about new thinking, together with a progressive and enterprising conception of the role brass bands should fill in a forward-looking age', fell victim to the rule in 1966.

This was an unsettled period which might easily have seen the total disappearance of the National Championships. However, although retired, Vaughan-Morris was invited by *The People* to continue in a freelance capacity to organize the national finals and the festival concert; and to regularize the uncertain situation in the regions, he took over the organization of the regional finals with the help of regional committees.

In December 1966, *The People* finally withdrew from the National Championships and handed them over to Vaughan-Morris, together with the trophies they had presented. An announcement stated: 'Throughout the long period of Odhams Press newspapers' association with the brass band movement, Mr E. Vaughan-Morris has been the administrator and producer on their behalf. His services to brass bands have rightly been fully acknowledged by the Movement for which he has done so much. The Directors of Odhams Press Newspapers Ltd are therefore sure that all associated with the Movement will be glad to know that arrangements have been completed whereby responsibility for organizing the Championships and Festival in their entirety has been passed to Vaughan-Morris who recently retired from Odhams and is now free of the many other calls upon his talents and time.'

That the valuable experience of Vaughan-Morris, along with his business and organizing abilities, was still to be utilized brought a certain relief to the band world and, under his leadership, the national and regional contests continued to develop over the next few years. The 1971 contests were the last he organized. The detailed organization had become an all-year responsibility and, having reached the age of 70, he felt it necessary to hand over his charge and to secure the continuation of the events on a long-term basis. The outcome of lengthy negotiations was the transfer of the championships to the company which published *The British Bandsman*, then operating from offices in London's Strand.

With an air of welcoming back the prodigal, *The British Bandsman*, announcing the change, said full responsibility for the championship and festival 'will once again be operated from 210 Strand, London. There is, of course, world wide familiarity in this address and there will be many advantages which can stem from these great and far reaching events being part of the family again'. Mr Peter Wilson, now editor of *The British Bandsman*, moved his home from Scotland to London to become organizing secretary of the events.

It was decided in 1973 to change the format of the championships by inviting only the previous year's winner: all other bands would have to qualify in the regional contest. About the same time Butlins, the holiday camp company, took over sponsorship of the National Youth Championships, which take place on the same day as the National Championships.

By 1975 more changes were afoot. The lease on 210 Strand had expired, and premises out of London were found. In August of that year, ownership of *The British Bandsman* passed to Robert D. Alexander, together with responsibility for the National Championships. A further change came two years later when ownership of the bandsman's newspaper passed to Rosehill Instruments Ltd, with Mr Alexander retaining, as he still does, responsibility for the championships. It was he who was responsible in 1978 for the introduction of the European championship, in which bands were invited from selected European countries to compete. Black Dyke Mills Band, under Major Peter Parkes, were the first winners, and held on to their title the following year, in which they also won the National Championship.

The contest diary is a very full one throughout the year. Since 1920 there has also been a spring festival at Belle Vue in May and in recent years the sponsorship of contests by commercial firms has become almost as fashionable as the sponsorship of a particular band. Fruit juice manufacturers, holiday camp concerns, fork-lift truck-makers and countless other concerns with no other direct connections with brass bands have come forward to sponsor contesting events. And, although the colliery band scene has changed since the nationalization of the coal industry, there are still enough colliery bands to support an annual contest at Blackpool in November for miners' bands.

Perhaps the most gruelling contests of all – and not only for the participating bandsmen but especially for the behind-the-scenes organizers – are the annual Whit Friday 'quickstep' contests, many of which date back a century and which have become a vital part of the brass band calendar. They are held in a dozen or more centres on the borders of Lancashire, Yorkshire and Cheshire and are still supported by hundreds of bandsmen and thousands of spectators and, in addition to providing the prize money, have, more importantly, raised thousands of pounds for charities. Physical endurance and good organization are as important in these contests as playing ability. Their history dates back to the Victorian era of Sunday School treats and the north country practice of an annual replacement of the best dress and suit at Whitsuntide, although this aspect is perhaps now long forgotten. Some of these annual gatherings and treats were linked with religious processions, headed by a brass band. Such was the demand for bands for this purpose that Lancastrian bandsmen had to be augmented by bandsmen from over the Yorkshire border. Changes in social habits have seen the demise of these traditional Whit walks and gatherings, which were formerly so much a part of the pattern of life in the industrial areas of the north. The introduction more recently of the Spring Bank Holiday has also had the effect of removing the old Whitsuntide feast from the calendar. But northerners, especially northern bandsmen, are often reluctant to accept change and for them the Whitsuntide festival, epitomized through the Whit Friday contests, lives on as an important date in their annual diary.

While some of the older contests have unfortunately been disbanded, others continue to flourish as enthusiastically as they did in their formative times. The contest at Stalybridge, where one of the early bands originated, is still functioning and will celebrate its centenary in 1982. Defunct contests have been replaced with new ones. Broad Oak, Ashton-under-Lyne, was a brand new venue in 1979.

These contests are ritualistic. Up to 39 bands – the giants of the brass band world as well as those who would be giant killers – separated by only minutes arrive by coach in a town, disembark with their instruments, then march and play their way along the village high street to the contest area where they play their chosen contest march. Then back to the coach and on to the next contest where the pattern is repeated. And so it goes on for five hours–a dozen or more times the ritual is performed. Up to 30,000 people have been known to attend the contests. On Whit Friday of 1939 Black Dyke Mills Band won a record seven firsts playing its own march *Queensbury*: in 1979 they gained five firsts, one second place and a third. Brighouse and Rastrick Band, their rivals, and Yorkshire Imperial Metals Band have both won six firsts.

With the original object of providing feast-day entertainment for workers and their families during a short respite from their labours no longer essential, a new object – of providing money for deserving local charities – has taken its place. Many of the organizers are not even active brass band enthusiasts except for that particular day, but are church or club officials who raise the money to finance the contests by way of cups and prize money through collections and raffles. They are imbued by a strong desire to maintain a long tradition peculiar to their part of the country in an age in which such things are all too often allowed to disappear. The organization is often in the hands of a small group of people–committees with no formal constitutions.

There have always been mixed feelings about the value of band contests. That they improve technique and musicianship and help keep up standards is beyond question. But against this is the argument that the elusive quality of musical communication through the composer is something that, unlike sporting events with which band contests are often compared, cannot be measured in points. And there is undoubtedly in contesting circles an obsession with 'form': much is made in programme notes and in the banding press of the past performances of bands taking part, the past travels on the brass band circuit of conductors (not infrequently a conductor has trained two bands taking part in the same contest, a situation which must raise the eyebrows of musicians in other spheres) and the value of the prizes. And in Yorkshire and the North West, where most of the bands still come from, there are long and convincing arguments that they are at a disadvantage because they come from regions that have numerous good bands compared with other regions where bands are spread more lightly over the area. Despite this inherent disadvantage, however, a study of the contests shows that it is invariably a band from one of these 'disadvantaged' areas that carries off the major prizes.

Contests, then, seem to be a necessary evil. Perhaps the organizers of the National Championships have got the menu right with their combination of contest and evening festival concert – the contest for the brass band purist, the festival for those who like the variety of the brass band repertoire.

Chapter Three

Conductors and Composers

All the time a familiar group of bands were jostling each other for the top positions at contests, a select group of conductors was also appearing regularly in the same lists. Whereas the borrowing of star players between bands was frowned upon and restrictions to prevent such unsportsmanlike activities eventually were placed upon them, there were no such inhibitions when it came to the professional conductors and band trainers. Throughout brass band history there has been a regular interchange on the rostrum. It is practised as frequently today as it was a century ago. Conductors transfer from band to band today with the same regularity as do football managers. Sometimes one finds them in the awkward position of training and conducting two or more bands for the same contest, and the situation verges on the ludicrous when the draw for play results in them mounting the rostrum on several successive occasions to conduct their different charges in the same test-piece.

For over 60 years from 1873 the most successful conductors could be counted on the fingers of one hand: John Gladney, who tops the lists with 20 successes at Belle Vue, Edwin Swift, Alexander Owen, William Rimmer and William Halliwell.

John Gladney was an Ulsterman, born in Belfast in 1839, and an accomplished woodwind instrumentalist during the 1860s with the Hallé Orchestra in Manchester. His brass band record would undoubtedly have been even more extraordinary had he turned his attention to this form of musical expression earlier in his career. He gave lessons to more than 100 bands and made many musical arrangements for them, but it was with Meltham Mills, Kingston Mills and Black Dyke Mills bands that he achieved most of his contest successes: seven with Black Dyke, including a double in 1902 by winning both the Open and the National Championships, six with Kingston Mills and four with Meltham Mills. He died in 1911. Black Dyke's history has already been described in Chapter One. Kingston Mills took its name from a cotton mill in Hyde, Cheshire, and was one of the premier bands of the last three decades of the century until it hit a bad patch after its last championship win in 1901. There is still a band in Hyde, re-formed in 1946. Meltham Mills, from Huddersfield, under Gladney's baton, was the first band to achieve a hat-trick at Belle Vue with three consecutive wins in 1876-1877, and 1878. Gladney's association with this band came about in a curious, but typically Yorkshire, way. He is said to have criticised its poor performance in a contest he was adjudicating in 1873. He was afterwards invited to meet the bandsmen so that they could express their feelings. He was then told by them that if he thought the band was so bad he could have the job of conducting them and improving their performance. To their suprise he accepted. One of a family of instrumentalists in the band at the time of their hat-trick, a trombonist called Edwin Stead, became a musical legend about whom stories are still recalled. He had a part in achieving another hat-trick in the following three years with Black Dyke Mills Band, a feat that no player has ever repeated. A band still flourishes there, now known as the Meltham and Meltham Mills Band.

Another of the members of the Meltham Mills Band at this period of Gladney's glory was also to become one of the formidably successful group of conductors: Alexander Owen. His early experience had been gained with the Stalybridge Old Band, which he had conducted at the early age of 16, but it was as a brilliant cornet player that he was recruited by Meltham Mills. He then became conductor of Black Dyke and was associated with a number of other famous bands in both Yorkshire and Lancashire. These were the days when bands were able to make their own choice of test-piece at most contests and Owen arranged many great musical works as 'selections' for brass band. His arrangement of *Reminiscences from Rossini* was played at no fewer than 27 contests and another of his selections, from Berlioz's *Damnation of Faust* was performed at 21 contests. He died in 1920, but his name is perpetuated through the award of an annual scholarship for players under the age of 18.

The third of the great and successful conductors during the final decades of the nineteenth century was Edwin Swift, a self-trained musician who joined a brass band in his home town of Linthwaite, near Huddersfield, at the tender age of ten. He later worked in a local mill and spent all his life among the weavers of the district. 'I am a weaver by trade and a musician by accident', he often remarked. He spent every available moment composing or arranging band music, using a primitive desk near his weaving loom and paying countless fines for damaged pieces of cloth that slipped through while his thoughts were on his music. He is reputed on one occasion in his teens to have visited the rehearsal of a rival band and committed to his memory and then scored for his own band their special new march – and forestalled them with its first public performance. He eventually drove himself too hard and suffered a serious breakdown in health, after which he gave up playing to concentrate on conducting. In 1874 his local Linthwaite Band was taking on the crack bands of the era: that year they won ten first prizes, including the Belle Vue championship. He was also associated with several other great bands, notably the Wyke Temperance Band. He became ill again and died in 1904.

These three men, then, ruled supreme in the bandroom and on the rostrum for the last 30 years of the century and had a profound influence on the band scene. How tight was their hold on the movement can be judged from the following statistics. Out of 18 bands taking part in the 1894 championships at Belle Vue five were conducted by Alexander Owen, five by Edwin Swift and four by John Gladney. They certainly had no inhibitions about not putting all their eggs in one basket.

The contesting careers and successes of Gladney and Owen overlapped into the new century – Gladney achieved a 'double' with Black Dyke in 1902 by taking first place at both Belle Vue and the new National Championship in London – but they were to give way to two younger conductors who were set to be equally dominant for the next 30 years: William Rimmer and William Halliwell.

Rimmer, who was born in 1862, started his career as cornetist in the Southport Rifles' Band from which he was recruited by Besses o' th' Barn Band, with whom he was soloist for several years, succeeding the legendary Fred Durham. He was in great demand as a band trainer and was associated with the Irwell Springs Band for 13 years from 1896. His conducting feats were prodigious. At one concert in 1897 he conducted all five winning bands and at another in his native Southport he conducted seven bands all of which won a prize. His distinguished record of successes included five consecutive 'doubles', leading the prize-winning band at both Belle Vue and the National Championships in

London every year from 1905 to 1909. Rimmer became music editor for the publishing firm of Wright & Round in 1913, composing and arranging a vast number of items many of which are still featured in brass band programmes. He died in 1936.

Rimmer must also have possessed great foresight. He was conductor of the Hebden Bridge Band – for which he was paid 8s. (40p) for a rehearsal and £1 for a contest – in 1909 when according to the band minute book records, it was decided 'that Harry Mortimer be given the spare cornet'. What a momentous decision that proved to be.

As a composer of brass band music, Rimmer was the idol of a young Welshman, Tom Powell, who was himself to earn a distinguished and respected place in the brass band movement, particularly in his native Wales. Until his sudden death in 1965, T.J. Powell was musical director for an astonishing 43 years of the Mellingriffith Works Band, one of the oldest and best known bands in Wales which traced its history back to the early years of the nineteenth century. The works closed down in 1967, but the band was later adopted as the Excelsior Ropes Works Band. It was, however, as a composer of marches that Powell was best known throughout the brass band fraternity. His compositions, many of them associated with the castles of Wales, earned him the title of the Souza of Wales.

Where Rimmer left off in the sphere of competitive conducting, William Halliwell took over and became the most successful band trainer and conductor for the next 25 years. He conducted all the great bands of the period – Hebden Bridge, Irwell Springs, Fodens, Wingates Temperance, Besses o' th' Barn, Brighouse and Rastrick, Black Dyke, Munn and Feltons among many others. He notched up 16 firsts at Belle Vue between 1910 and 1936 and ten National Championships, completing the double on no less than nine occasions.

Another legendary name among brass bands during this period, of which there are still echoes, was that of J. Ord Hume who, in a career spanning over half a century, became a prolific arranger of brass band music. Born in Edinburgh in 1864, he had been cornet soloist in a military band, the Royal Scots Greys. It was his arrangement of *Gems from Sullivan's Operas* that was chosen as the test-piece for the first of the National Championships in London in 1900. He and another famous arranger, Lieutenant Charles Godfrey, were between them responsible for most of the brass band repertoire at this time. It was a type of music that became particularly associated with brass bands and which, despite criticisms from more modern enthusiasts, still has many defenders and still appears in concert programmes.

By 1930 the famous Mortimer family had arrived firmly on the brass band scene. While William Halliwell with Besses and Brighouse and Rastrick was still reigning in Manchester, father Fred Mortimer was achieving success after success in the 'National' in London with Foden's Motor Works Band where he had succeeded Halliwell. Throughtout the 1930s he scored seven first prizes in London with the band, twice having three successive wins. Mortimer had an unusual feature in that he conducted with his left hand. This apparently dated back to the days when he both played and conducted, playing the cornet with his right hand and conducting with his left.

By the 1940s and 1950s it was his eldest son Harry Mortimer who had achieved eminence as a conductor. His contesting career as trainer and conductor was a most distinguished one, with nine firsts at Belle Vue and ten in the National Championships, nine of which were consecutive wins. He gave up competitive conducting in the 1950s but is still in his late seventies very much a part of the movement that has been his life, promoting the British Open at Belle Vue and making frequent appearances as a concert conductor. Such was the response to a television programme in which Men of Brass, a combination he formed of instrumentalists from several of the leading bands, played some of his favourite brass band music, that it had to be repeated. With a keen eye on the future of the movement, he is an enthusiastic supporter of the National Youth Brass Band and in 1978 at Belle Vue provided them with their first major platform.

Harry Mortimer is now the dominant personality of the movement and there is no question that his efforts have been to a large extent responsible for the raising of the status and today's popularity of brass bands. During the 1930s when he was playing principal trumpet with the Hallé and Liverpool Philharmonic Orchestras he got to know many of the great orchestral conductors and through these contacts and friendships was able to persuade some of the leading conductors – men such as Sir Hamilton Harty, Sir Adrian Boult, Sir Arthur Bliss and Sir Malcolm Sargent – to conduct and compose for brass bands. He once recalled in a conversation with the author how he considered playing the trumpet in these famous orchestras had been a great advantage to him. Whereas there were large numbers of violinists and other instrumentalists, there were only two or sometimes three trumpeters and the conductor, therefore, got to know the trumpet

Harry Mortimer, doyen of the brass band movement, admires the Ivor Novello award he received in 1978 for his work for brass bands.

(Photo by courtesy of *The Times*)

players better. There was at that period, he recalled, a class distinction in the musical world. Brass bands, he added, had nothing to be ashamed of, but it was a time when they were frowned upon by the rest of the musical world. Their working-class origins resulted in an antipathy towards them which had slowly and gradually been broken down, particularly when composers such as Holst, Elgar and Ireland wrote for the brass band. 'These works were written specially for us and afterwards transcribed for the orchestra – and that was the opposite to what had previously been the case', he said.

Harry Mortimer may well be the last of that breed of conductors who dominated the arena. That is not to belittle the standards of his successors, but their task is more difficult now that more musicians in the brass band world are becoming professional conductors. Since Harry Mortimer's long run of wins, conductors have been less consistently successful in recent years. Part of the reason may be due to the more itinerant nature of their calling nowadays, for there are frequent changes and movements of musical directors and conductors, compared with conductors in the past who, although training a number of bands, tended to be more permanent in their conducting engagements. And, perusing contest results, one sees that for whatever reason successive wins are much less easy to come by than in former years. A band which reaches the top one year may be well down the lists or even unplaced the next. In recent years, apart from Leonard Lamb who had three successes at Belle Vue with Fairey Motor Works Band and won the National Championship in 1965, the most consistent conductor has been Major Peter Parkes with Black Dyke Mills Band's two successive wins in 1976 and 1977 at Belle Vue, a hat-trick in the national in 1975-1976, and 1977, the first European championship in 1978, and a double in 1979 by again winning the National and retaining their European title.

Otherwise, the only comparable consistency with that of the past has been in the mineworkers' annual contests when George Thompson with the Grimethorpe Colliery Band achieved three successive wins in 1967, 1968, and 1969. Major H. A. Kenney also completed a hat-trick with the Cory Band in 1970, 1971 and 1972 – in 1971 they also won the Granada Band of the Year award – and in 1974 he conducted them when they won the National and shared first place in the mineworkers' contest.

Composing for the brass band is not easy, since the instrumentation lacks a wide range of colour. The present form of instrumentation became established in the 1860s, and, apart from improvements in instruments affecting their tone, has remained virtually unchanged. Suggestions are mooted from time to time of variations in instrumentation which would afford more freedom to composers: the addition of extra trombones, more horns, even the use of trumpets. But bandsmen and brass band enthusiasts are slow to change. It has taken almost 150 years for the inclusion of percussion and that has been unacceptable to many of the older purists in the movement: others grudgingly accept it in concert work while regretting its appearance in contests. But such is progress within the movement in modern times that some of these changes may well be gradually introduced as more *avant-garde* music is accepted.

In its formative years the brass band was restricted to a repertoire in which selections from popular songs, often the music of light shows, were strung together, and solo items of the 'air with variations' type of music were the staple diet. Faced with this limitation and a lack of appreciation of the musical ability of many of these amateur bands, established and more distinguished composers failed to grasp the opportunities the medium presented. It was not until they were introduced directly to it that they realized the musical capabilities of what had by then become a vast and nationwide musical form, isolated thought it still was from the musical establishment. Once aware of the movement and its musical potential, composers became almost overwhelming in their enthusiasm and praise. Despite the lack of original music for brass band by already established composers, a sizeable repertoire of music from the pens of lesser known composers was being established. The movement has to thank the contesting side of the brass band world for encouraging the writing of original music in the form of test-pieces, many of which have become established favourites in any brass band programme.

Most of the credit for encouraging new musical compositions has gone to John Henry Iles, who began commissioning test-pieces in 1913. But the man who urged him to do so and who rightly deserves some of the credit, Herbert Whitely, has had his contribution in this respect underestimated. Whitely had been brought up in brass band country in Yorkshire where, during the 1890s, he was organist and choirmaster at Saddleworth Parish Church. He also pioneered from his home, postal courses for bandsmen in musical theory. In 1906 he became musical adviser to Iles and editor of *The British Bandsman* the specialized periodical for bandsmen which had been conceived in 1887 by Samuel Cope and was subsequently owned by Iles. Whitely remained editor until illness forced him to resign in 1930. He used the columns of his periodical and his influence with Henry Iles to urge the development of original brass band music. His achievement in persuading Iles probably did more than any other single factor to enhance the wider acceptance of the brass band and the realization of its musical capabilities.

For his benevolence in commissioning new works Iles has been described as the fairy godmother of brass band music. It was Whitely who supplied the magic wand. He also brought the new works to a wider audience by publishing them in his periodical. If established orchestral composers were slow to take up the opportunities, the writing of brass band music has brought distinction and renown on others who have specialized in writing for this musical medium.

Percy Fletcher was the first composer to be commissioned to write a test-piece for the National Championship. For the Crystal Palace contest of 1913 he wrote a tone poem entitled *Labour and Love* which put into a musical context two of the virtues of the movement. This and some of his subsequent compositions have become favourites among bandsmen: his *Epic Symphony*, written as the test-piece for the 1926 contest in London was also used as a test-piece on two subsequent occasions in 1938 and 1951.

The second composer to receive a commission was Cyril Jenkins who, for unfortunate reasons, secured a place for himself in brass band history. He wrote *Coriolanus* as the 1914 national test-piece, but the contest was cancelled because of the outbreak of war and he had to wait until 1920 before it was played in the National Championship. His best-known brass band composition, however, came the following year with *Life Divine* which created a stir at the time – some bandsmen claimed it was too difficult – but has since become a popular test-piece in other contests and on the concert platform. It is an ideal test-piece, abounding in trills and runs. Jenkins originally gave the piece the title of *A Comedy of Errors* but changed it on the advice of his publishers, who considered the original title might be too apposite, particularly in the early stages of rehearsal. Jenkins had decided to write a piece that was technically more difficult than his earlier composition. Before the contest many experienced bandmasters predicted he had carried out his intentions so effectively that the work would prove impossible to perform. After the contests experts reckoned that the study involved in its performance had improved technique by 25 per cent in the case of the best bands and that of the worst by 100 per cent. It is a work that has become associated, because of the number of occasions on which he has conducted it, with Harry Mortimer. As a tribute on his 75th birthday in 1977 he was invited to conduct it at the festival concert in the Royal Albert Hall which followed the annual championships. Harry Mortimer, discussing this particular piece of music with the author, commented: 'It is a piece that impressed me. It is a declaratory, descriptive piece of music, although it is difficult for one band alone to play: it is too strenuous. It is better with massed bands and as I nowadays do most of that sort of conducting I suppose it has become especially associated with me. I often get my leg pulled about it', he admitted. 'When we are considering a programme people say "I suppose you will be conducting *Life Divine*". I tell them that life has been divine for me', added the man who once described himself as 'the happiest conductor in the world' – a description that befits him both on and off the podium.

Two further test-pieces came from the pen of Cyril Jenkins, who died in 1978 at the age of 94: *Victory* which was performed at the 1929 contest in London, and *Saga of the North*, used as the British Open championship test-piece at Belle Vue in 1965. This latter piece, however, has proved less popular than his earlier works.

Henry Gheel was another composer who came to be particularly associated with brass bands as both composer and adjudictor, although he had originally had ambitions of becoming a concert pianist. His first brass band composition *Oliver Cromwell* was written as a test-piece in 1923 and he followed it a year later with *On the Cornish Coast*. His other works, some of which still figure in brass band concert programmes, included *Sinfonietta Pastorale*, *In Tudor Days* and *Festival Overture*.

Around the same period Denis Wright came to prominence in the brass band sphere as a composer with his tone poem *Joan of Arc*, the 1925 test-piece. Two years later he wrote another, *The White Rider* and, after the Second World War, *Overture for an Epic Occasion*. Wright was a pioneer of massed brass band concerts, using the bands in massed formation rather than keeping each band as a separate unit. His other important contribution to the brass movement was his founding in 1951 of the National Youth Brass Band which has provided the movement with some of its finest young players. The band meets twice a year for a week's course under distinguished conductors from both the brass band and orchestral worlds. Over 100 young musicians take part in each course. Admission to the band is by audition, for which there is a long waiting list.

These composers, however, were men who distinguished themselves through their brass band work. The movement, despite Iles's efforts, had to wait until 1928 before an already distinguished orchestral composer turned his attention in the direction of brass bands. That composer was Gustav Holst. His emergence as a composer of brass band music was a notable and widely acclaimed point in the movement's history. Others began to express amazement at the vastness of this branch of musical life which was so bound up with the existence and aspirations of a large mass of the musical population in the industrial and mining regions of the country and elsewhere. Holst's original work for brass band, his *Moorside Suite*, was the test-piece for the 1928 National Championship. He had an interesting brass background, which was to prove of inestimable value in his compositions for brass band. In 1895 he had been awarded an open scholarship for composition at the Royal College of Music and in order to supplement his scholarship he played trombone in various orchestras for several years. It was a fortunate experience which provided him with an intimate knowledge of the capabilities of the instruments of the orchestra, particularly those of the brass section. His daughter, Imogen Holst, who has herself written for the brass band, has said that this experience taught her father far more than he would every have gleaned from text-books and was one of the most important things that happened to him during his years of training at the college.

By 1909 Holst was writing for military bands. His first *Suite for Military Band* written that year was, in his daughter's opinion, 'Superbly written . . . it must have been a startling change from the usual operatic selections and there are bandsmen who still remember the excitement of the first rehearsal in 1909. In spite of its original approach, the Suite never breaks away from the essential traditions of the band, and the March is the sort of music that is beloved of bombardons and euphoniums.' This was followed by a *Second Suite for Military Band* composed two years later.

Holst's *Moorside Suite* has three movements: scherzo, nocturne and march, and bears traces of the folk-song settings that he had composed 20 years earlier. 'The music has vitality', says Imogen Holst. 'It looks forward as well as back. There is a rare tenderness in the opening of the nocturne and the last movement is like a mature comment on the early *Marching Song* of 1906; it is a fitting acknowledgement of a twenty years' debt of gratitude for the solid and companionable help that folk songs had brought him.'

Holst preferred writing for the brass band rather than for military bands. He found the brass band mellower and more flexible. At Crystal Palace he heard his *Suite* played 15 times by successive bands. What impressed him about the experience was the extraordinary enthusiasm by the amateur bandsmen combined with the skill of professionals. 'It was not only the technical proficiency that he admired so much: it was their sense of phrasing and their real musicianship', says Imogen Holst.* He became a propagandist in the campaign to make better music available to brass bands: to diversify from the inevitable 'selection from . . .' and to persuade composers that brass bands were not something to be avoided.

Progressive bandmasters were becoming increasingly dissatisfied with the staple repertoire of the gems from Gounod and selections from Sullivan type of music. Holst's contribution was significant: no composer of such repute had hitherto turned his attention to the brass band. Even so, the musical establishment was slow to follow his example. It was another two years before the next significant event took place. This time it was no less a musical notability than Edward Elgar who threw his weight behind the brass band movement.

Elgar was proudly provincial, a factor which may help to explain his great interest in brass bands. He frequently denigrated what he considered to be the smugness of official musical life and as early as 1903 he was saying that 'some day the Press will awaken to the fact, already known abroad and to some few of us in England, that the living centre of music in Great Britain is not London but somewhere farther north'. He was not unaware of the part that brass bands were playing in that centre of provincial music to which he alluded.

A selection from Elgar's cantata *Caractacus* had been the test-piece at Belle Vue in 1903, the year significantly in which he was referring elsewhere to provincial music-making. Twenty-seven years later he was invited to write the test-piece for the 1930 championship in London. He responded with his *Severn Suite*. Elgar was unable to attend its performance because of illness, but George Bernard Shaw, to whom he had dedicated it, was there at Crystal Palace. He heard it played by several of the bands and complimented at least one on its performance. Elgar's other mus-

**The Music of Gustav Holst* by Imogen Holst. 2nd edn (Oxford University Press, 1968).

ical contribution to the movement is the brass band arrangement of the ninth of his *Enigma Variations* – Nimrod – a firm favourite still with bandsmen. Sir Adrian Boult, who has himself often expressed appreciation of the tonal quality of brass bands, has recalled how Elgar once surprised him by asking whether he had ever heard a good brass band. The conductor had to admit that, although he hailed from Lancashire with its historic associations with banding, he had not at that time, although he rectified the omission later. Elgar had gone on to describe how he had recently heard a brass band playing an arrangement of his Second Symphony. It had been considerably shortened but still gave a good idea of the material it contained – and, he had added, 'the way those cornets tackled my string passages was quite extraordinary'.

Elgar had already made several sketches for a suite when he was invited to write the 1930 test-piece. His acceptance marked a turning-point for brass bands: for a composer of Elgar's stature to produce a work especially written for the brass band was an important step forward in the musical world. The tables had been turned: instead of arrangements of an orchestral work for the brass band, here an original brass band work had been produced which was later arranged for military bands (by Henry Gheel, whom Elgar had consulted on the original scoring) and, two years later, rewritten by Elgar himself for performance by a full orchestra at the Worcester Festival in 1932.

Elgar's own practical experience as a musician – he was also a skilled performer on the trombone in his younger days – had made him aware of the potential in brass band instrumentation.

His contribution to the brass band repertoire provided encouragement to other composers. Peter Warlock, music critic of *The Daily Telegraph*, for instance, claimed it was high time the brass band was recognized as a musical combination of real artistic importance. In many an industrial town, he wrote, it was the only medium through which music entered the lives of the people. He criticized Grove's *Dictionary of Music* for ignoring 'this great national movement' and its prime mover, Henry Iles – an omission Grove subsequently rectified. Warlock declared that the finest brass players were to be found not in the military bands but in the mine and the factory. The brass band movement was essentially democratic and was destined to play a significant part in the musical life of the country. The quality of the average brass band programme, however, left much to be desired. No musical combination was so badly in need of original compositions and of artistically scored arrangements of other good music. 'At present,' he added, 'there is a lamentable lack of enterprise on the part of our publishers: operatic pot-pouris and showy Victorian cornet solos still predominate in their brass band catalogues.'

Everyone agreed that for too long a period the brass band had been neglected, even ignored, as a legitimate and serious form of musical expression. Most people, apart from the enthusiasts, still regarded it as a rather jolly, outdoor entertainment, chiefly associated with the park, pier or promenade bandstand, some of its instruments too closely aligned with the vision of street musicians playing *The Lost Chord* or the little groups of Salvation Army musicians providing backing for the hymns. But, it seemed, a new era was dawning. The example of Holst and Elgar and the exhortations of some of the music critics would surely bear fruit.

The next composer of distinction to turn his attention to the brass band was John Ireland, who produced his *Downland Suite* as the championship test-piece in 1932. That, and his later composition, the *Comedy Overture*, are still popular pieces, as they have been among successive generations of bandsmen. Like Elgar's *Severn Suite*, Ireland's *Downland Suite* was afterwards used by the composer in his *London Overture* for orchestra. But brass bandsmen did not mind that: Ireland, and Elgar, they considered had got their priorities right.

During the 1930s other distinguished orchestral composers were invited to write test-pieces: Sir Granville Bantock and Dr Herbert Howells among them. The brass band appeared to be a source of inspiration for modern composers, but in reality it was only in providing specially commissioned test-pieces for contests, valuable though they were, that composers of standing were contributing to the brass band repertory. The sparse literature of the brass band was otherwise not being extended. There were a number of reasons for this apparent neglect: unlike Holst and Elgar, many orchestral composers lacked the practical knowledge of the techniques of brass instruments, while others regarded them as old-fashioned and restricted. Not all the fault was that of composers. Brass band musicians tended to look with suspicion – some of them, indeed, still do – at compositions which deviated from their traditional style: they often lacked the breadth of musical vision and encouragement that would enable them to experiment.

The exhortations to composers and the musical enthusiast continued. Sir Landon Ronald, in a newspaper article published in 1933, regretted that the musical community was divided into self-contained sections. He confessed to his own amazement at the extent of brass band activity – over 100,000 men in some 5,000 bands. 'I do not see how any musician can fail to be impressed by this widespread, enthusiastic amateur movement in music ... Practically all these are identified with collieries or factories. There is no doubt whatever that they form a branch of music in which this country is without rival and it is good to hear that such composers as Elgar, Bantock, Holst and Ireland have awakened to the fact that here is a wonderful field for them.'

Three years later, J. H. Elliott, northern music critic of the *News Chronicle* and co-author of *The Brass Band Movement* reported that the brass band was emerging slowly into a place in the sun only by virtue of the new brass music. As long as the all-brass ensemble was confined to 'arrangements' of music conceived in terms of other media, it was 'employing a foreign tongue without possessing the natural advantage of a native, while its own rich and resourceful language remained undeveloped – indeed largely unsuspected,' he wrote. It had to be admitted, he added, that the repertory of the average brass band, despite the existence of these original works, was still cluttered with antediluvian operatic selections as well as a good deal that was entirely trivial.

If bandmasters and bandsmen were loath to indulge in too much experimentation, it is true also that the public listening to the brass band also had some responsibility for the situation – and bandmasters naturally took cognizance of their tastes. In general they were reasonably well satisfied with the musical fare that brass bands provided. In these pre-war years, the brass band was still mainly an outdoor form of musical entertainment, and the holidaymaker sitting in his deckchair on the pier or promenade or pausing to listen to the band as he strolled around the park on a summer Sunday afternoon was not receptive to the unfamiliar.

Sir Granville Bantock was another of the distinguished composers who turned his attention towards brass bands at this period. In 1930 his *Oriental Rhapsody* was written as the Belle Vue test-piece and he followed it three years later with *Prometheus Unbound* for the London championship. Dr Herbert Howells, another well-known orchestral composer, produced a brass band test-piece, *Pageantry*, used at Belle Vue in 1934 and in London three years later. Sir Arthur Bliss, also impressed at the high standard of these amateur bandsmen, made an important contribution to the brass band repertoire with his *Kenilworth Suite*, which was the test-piece at Crystal Palace in 1936 (the last to be written for that popular venue before it was destroyed by fire), and it has remained through the intervening years a great favourite with bandsmen and audiences. It has three movements and is based on a visit by Elizabeth I to Kenilworth Castle in 1575. The brass movement had to wait until 1963 for his other notable brass composition, the *Belmont Variations*.

Firstly Holst, then Elgar and Bantock, followed by Ireland, Howells and Bliss: a distinguished company of composers whose original contributions brought undoubted respect to the movement and were hailed as important milestones in the history of brass bands, marking the movement's release from the past isolation. By then, the *Musical Times* was proclaiming that the brass band had 'become recognised as a truly musical combination and not a mere cheerful outside entertainer'. The brass band was said to have arrived. But important though it was, the contribution of these distinguished composers did not at the time please all brass band enthusiasts. These works to many who had been brought up with the traditional repertoire represented new and unfamiliar sounds.

No other distinguished orchestral composers were to produce original works for brass band for two decades and, even then, the supply was meagre – Bliss's *Belmont Variations* and Ralph Vaughan Williams's *Variations for Brass Band*, written in 1957. Of this latter composition, *The Times* said: 'It is no exaggeration to say that this is the finest piece of music ever written for brass band even though other English composers of eminence have contributed to the development by writing for this essentially unwieldy medium.' A previously unknown work by Vaughan Williams, an overture entitled *Henry V* apparently composed for brass band around 1933 or 1934, was discovered in 1980 by Howard Snell, conductor of Desford Colliery Band, as he browsed through a catalogue of the composer's works.

Young composers during the 1930s continued to ignore the exhortations and the lead of these eminent composers. During the war there were no contests for which to compose in London, although the Belle Vue contests continued when bands for two years at any rate were allowed a choice of test-piece. After the war, however, a new generation of composers were to make considerable reputations for themselves within the movement with some fine and lasting works – Eric Ball, who has been as prolific in composing sacred music for the Salvation Army as he has secular music for contesting bands, Gilbert Vinter, Denis Wright, who has enhanced his earlier reputation, and Frank Wright, whose arrangements have been much praised.

Eric Ball is the most outstanding brass band composer, and the quantity of his output has not detracted from the quality of his work. His list of compositions is phenomenal: for the brass band he has written well over 60 original works and marches and in the region of 30 arrangements. He is the most outstanding example also of the close ties between secular bands and the Salvation Army. In addition to his vast output for secular bands, he has also written more than 70 works for performance by the Salvation Army, several of which are viewed enviously by the contesting band world.

One of his early introductions to music was by way of band concerts in the park: the traditional repertoire introduced Ball to music he would not otherwise have heard at the time, because he then was unable to afford to attend orchestral concerts. He tends, therefore, to be less critical than some other composers of the arrangements of operatic selections which formed such a staple in the musical fare of that period. He was brought up in a Salvation Army atmosphere and although he had ambitions of becoming a cathedral organist he went instead into the Salvation Army's music department, where the reading of submitted scores formed part of his duties. While he was there he started composing himself and formed one of the Army's most famous ensembles, the S.P. and S. (Salvationist Publishing and Supplies) Band and later conducted the International Staff Band. He left his full-time work with the Salvation Army during the Second World War. A meeting with that influential figure in the brass band movement, John Henry Iles, resulted in his appointment as editor of *The British Bandsman* and an invitation to write his first brass band test-piece, *Salute to Freedom*. It was in this post-war period that Ball took up conducting, first with the Brighouse and Rastrick Band with whom he won the 'National' in 1946 and later the C.W.S. (Manchester) Band, the former Ransome and Marles Band and City of Coventry. While regarding contests as an essential feature of banding, he preferred concert work and is still, in his seventies, in demand as a conductor and composter and an adjudicator at contests.

Dr Thomas Keighley was the composer to whom the organizers of the Belle Vue championships turned when they decided in 1925, like their London contemporaries, to commission original compositions as test-pieces. It consolidated a close association between Dr Keighley and the Belle Vue contests, for he was invited to write the test-piece on no fewer than six occasions during the decade up to his death in 1935 at the age of 65. His works generally had either a Shakespearean theme or a strongly northern flavour. He was born in 1869 in sound brass band country, Stalybridge in Cheshire, and had worked in cotton mills before taking up music professionally. His interest in music had been aroused by the Stalybridge Old Band who in those days were a powerful contesting band. He became a lecturer in music at Manchester University and was later professor of organ and composition at the Royal Manchester College of Music. In 1980 his work underwent a revival when his composition *The Crusaders*, a symphonic rhapsody based on Sir Walter Scott's novel *The Talisman*, which he wrote originally for the British Open Championship in 1932, was chosen as the test-piece for the Grand Shield section of the Belle Vue Spring Festival.

Gilbert Vinter's earliest brass band work, *Salute to Youth* was produced in 1961, and was commissioned as the test-piece in the regional qualifying contests that year. There followed *Variations on a Ninth* in 1964 and a more abstract piece, *Triumphant Rhapsody*, which was the national test-piece in 1965; many musicians believe his *Symphony of Marches* to be his finest score. *The Trumpets*, the first performance of which Vinter conducted, was commissioned to mark the completion of the Royal Festival Hall in London and is one of the few original works for brass band and chorus, 'combing those two great amateur movements in music-making – the brass band and the choral society', Vinter said at the time. It is now performed infrequently. Many of Vinter's shorter and lighter pieces and quartets have become better known than his test-pieces. In 1968 he composed three main pieces, *Vizcaya*, one of his less successful works which resembles the *Carnaval Romain* by Berlioz, *John O'Gaunt*, a concert overture which has become one of his most popular compositions, and *Entertainments*, a light-hearted suite of three movements which was originally written for string orchestra and later scored for brass band. In 1969, the last year of his life, Vinter wrote two major works which were commissioned as test-pieces: *Spectrum*, for the Belle Vue contest, in which he portrays in music the seven colours of the spectrum, and *James Cook, Circumnavigator* for the New Zealand championships.

Eric Ball and Gilbert Vinter are both synonymous with what band enthusiasts regard as good brass band music and rarely is a concert programme assembled without the inclusion of their works.

The commissioning of special compositions was initially confined to works for bands in the championship section of contests, but this policy has gradually been extended and works are now commissioned for all grades in contests as well as for the festival concerts that take place annually at the Royal Albert Hall after the National Championships. Although the commissioning of special works was felt to be important, there were many – and still are – who regarded transcription as a source of enrichment of the brass band repertoire. One of these was the distinguished music critic of *The Times* who quoted the example of the late Sir Malcolm Sargent's transcription of Mozart's F Minor *Fantasia* as providing a new high watermark in brass band music when it was first performed in 1946. ' . . . bandsmen will find in it music of the finest kind which will exercise them in the virtues of crisp attack and brilliance of execution, in variety of tone colour, in the fugal style and in the melodic flexibility which they already possess in a high degree. In Mozart's *Fantasia* the brass band has annexed a piece that it may with perfect propriety make peculiarly its own', he wrote.

In the 1960s new conductors emerged bringing with them new approaches to brass band music. This coincided with a *renaissance* in brass band popularity, not only among its traditional audiences but among followers of classical music. This latter development was evidenced by the growing number of invitations to brass bands to take part in some of the major music festivals and through the commissions for new music paid for by grants from the Arts Council.

A new generation of composers became interested in the medium, many of them young composers or music students, who brought new musical techniques to their compositions – often techniques for which traditional audiences were unprepared. Scottish composers were prominent among the newcomers: Martin Dalby, who wrote his *Music for a Brass Band* while he was still a student at the Royal College of Music in 1962; Thea Musgrave, whose *Variations for Brass Band* brought a different sound, and Thomas Wilson's equally unfamiliar *Sinfonietta*. Edward Gregson also started writing for brass bands while he was still a student at the Royal College of Music: much of his music has been compared to that of Gilbert Vinter.Much of the music of the 1970s has been far removed from the traditional repertoire, and as a result the movement has been beset with controversy in recent years. It is significant that much of the newer music has been composed for concert performance rather than as contest test-pieces. Some of it has had a hostile reception and, indeed, has hardened attitudes of many a brass band audience against contemporary or *avant-garde* music. Most conductors are careful to vary their programmes with a deft mixture of new and traditional. This was notably the case when Black Dyke Mills Band and Grimethorpe Colliery Bands were invited to take part in the Henry Wood Promenade Concerts in 1974 ('Brass bands are a Yorkshire tradition and much serious and good music has been written for them', said Sir Robert Ponsonby, music controller at the BBC explaining the invitation); their programme consisted of Elgar's *Severn Suite*, Holst's *Moorside Suite* and *The Grimethorpe Aria*, an uncompromising new work commissioned for the Grimethorpe Band from Harrison Birtwhistle – a work that was certainly different and at first not enthusiastically received by bandsmen themselves, let alone the audiences. However, many bandsmen are not averse to accepting a challenge and Birtwhistle's music, like some of the works of other contemporary composers, was certainly that. Paul Patterson is another young composer whose work is controversial: his *Chromascope* was commissioned by Besses o' th' Barn and was first performed at the Harrogate Festival in 1974, and another of his works, *Cataclysm*, gives an unusual amount of free expression to the players. It was described as being 'light years removed from traditional band writing'.

William Mathias made a useful addition to the repertoire with his *Vivat Regina*, written for the Queen's Silver Jubilee and first performed at the Royal Albert Hall in June 1977 and recorded by the Black Dyke Mills Band.

Another of the new generation of composers is Arthur Butterworth, a composer whose strong northern connections are expressed in some of his works, such as *A Dales Suite* and *Path Across the Moors*. His *Symphonic Study* is a highly imaginative and accomplished piece of brass band writing.

Perhaps the most prolific of the modern composers is Gordon Langford, whose work covers many differing musical avenues and whose assocation with brass bands began in the late 1960s. His particular instrument is the trombone and his musical activities have included playing in a military band, dance bands, and the D'Oyly Carte Opera Company orchestra. Surprisingly, he has never played in a brass band. There is rarely a brass band programme compiled nowadays, however, that does not include at least one of his compositions or arrangements. While appreciating so-called 'modern' music, he believes audiences like a good melody and that brass band music does not have to be difficult to be rewarding for both players and audiences.

Much of the credit for encouraging this new music has to go to

Elgar Howarth, the conductor, arranger and composer, who has almost revolutionized the repertoire since he became musical director of the Grimethorpe Colliery Band in 1972. Howarth, whose reputation in the orchestral world is international, has a strong brass band background. His early musical life was as a cornet player in Eccles, Lancashire, where his father was bandmaster of a local band. He went on to play trumpet with some of the major orchestras and chamber ensembles. This background established a great respect in him for the brass band, but he realized that its repertoire was completely divorced from the mainstream of music, particularly contemporary music. He set about convincing contemporary composers that the brass band was worth composing for and, at the same time, convincing bandsmen that the unfamiliar sound of *avant-garde* music was good music, and within their capabilities as performers. He invited composers to hear the Grimethorpe miners play; they went away impressed by the players' abilities and returned with their commissions: Derek Bourgeois, a former tuba player, who has written several pieces for Grimethorpe is a composer with a strong musical sense of humour but whose works are demanding for the players; Hans Werner Henze, a young German composer whose *Ragtime and Habaneras*, written for Grimethorpe in 1975, is greatly admired by bandsmen; and Toru Takemitsu, a Japanese composer, whose *Garden Rain* provided another new musical experience. Howarth's own works have also made an important contribution. His *Fireworks*, written as the 1975 test-piece in the British Open championship, is a guide to instruments of the brass band, including a wide range of percussion equipment which, in itself, was something of a revolution in the brass band world. Percussion now forms an important part of brass band instrumentation, after being precluded from the scene for most of banding's history. Apart from its wide use in Elgar Howarth's *Fireworks*, a number of other recent works make a feature of percussion, including Phyllis Tate's *Illustrations*, and Buxton Orr's *Concerto* for *Trumpet and Brass Band*, in which the percussion part is an important element of the work.

Despite the tendency of brass band traditionalists to prefer the music of the past to that of the present, Howarth has a musical sense of humour, writing lighter novelty pieces under the name of W. Hogarth Lear, an anagram of his own name. His confidence in contemporary music is bringing rewards. Other leading bands are becoming less sceptical and are now experimenting with the new sounds and increasingly including them in their programmes.

Another conductor who has actively encouraged new music is Geoffrey Brand, particularly in his capacity from 1967 to 1975 as music adviser to the National Youth Brass Band and latterly as conductor of the National Youth Brass Band of Scotland, as well as a conductor of several championship bands.

Young players have fewer prejudices than their elders and it is significant that much contemporary music has initially been performed by these two bands and other youth bands. Their ability to do so speaks highly of the improved standards of musicianship. For example, Elgar Howarth's *Mosaic* written in 1956 for a light music festival but disqualified because it was thought to be too difficult is now often performed by youth bands.

Chapter Four

Bands in the twentieth century

As the twentieth century arrived, brass bands were, with the possible exception of choral singing, the largest amateur force in the national musical life. And they remained the possession of the working classes. These were still the days of outdoor entertainment: gala parades, Sunday school treats, seaside music and concerts in the public parks. Bands were much in demand to lead these processions or provide light entertainment for Sunday concerts on the bandstand. In numbers, support and popularity the brass band movement had reached its full height. What was to follow in the years ahead was a series of devastating blows that were calculated to threaten the survival of any movement, however strong.

The first of these was the outbreak of the First World War in 1914. Inevitably, as large numbers of men went off to fight the number of bands declined. Others struggled for survival, held together tenuously by older stalwarts. Instruments were put into storage. In some instances, like that of the Musselburgh and Fishberrow Trades Band from Scotland, the entire band enlisted *en bloc*. Just how disastrous the effect of the war was going to be was soon evident from the casualty lists. Over six million men served in the British Armed Forces. By the end of the war nearly one million had been killed, of whom 750,000 came from the United Kingdom. Many more suffered injury or the effects of gassing. How extensive was the total effect of the war on the brass band movement is impossible to estimate in numerical terms. Band journals published rolls of honour regularly but these were undoubtedly incomplete. Hundreds of bandsmen were among the dead or injured. Some bands were decimated: others were disastrously reduced in their membership when the cost in human terms was counted at the end of the war. Many bands were unable to overcome the serious losses in manpower and never revived. Surviving bandsmen returned home on their demobilization to find no band left with which to play. Other bands that were badly depleted merged with those of neighbouring districts.

But the situation was not entirely hopeless and bandsmen were endowed with a strong spirit and sense of survival. The contests at Belle Vue had continued throughout the war years with difficulty. The prize lists of the period indicate the nature of the war effort of the civilians who were left behind: colliery bands, railwaymen and motor workers generally. In London things were different. Crystal Palace, centre for the National Championship, was occupied by the Government departments throughout the war and the departure of the civil servants took some time: it was not until 1920 that the way was cleared for a resumption of the championship. Even then there was a forewarning of the harsh industrial climate looming over the country in the next few years: the effects of a miners' strike prevented 25 colliery bands out of the total entry of 113 bands from taking part in the resumed contest.

The miners were to be in the forefront of industrial trouble over the next few years. Faced with the threat of a national miners' strike in 1919, the Government had appointed a commission to investigate the situation in the mines. When the Government failed to act on the commission's recommendations, the miners felt deceived and went on strike. They were in dispute again in 1921 over a proposed reduction in their wages and it was further trouble in this respect – a proposal by the colliery owners to reduce wages and at the same time increase working hours – that ultimately led to the General Strike of 1926.

The 1920s were years of consolidation for brass bands rather than growth. There were now considerably fewer bands and some of the former players were finding other ways of occupying their leisure time without deserting their families for the bandroom. It was a natural reaction when four years of their life had been spent away from home. The gramophone and the wireless were also being developed and offered new opportunities to listen to music at home. It was ironic that one of the main reasons for the growth of brass bands in their early years, the productive use of leisure time, was becoming partly responsible for the decline of bands at this later period. Increased facilities for travel, another of the factors in the early growth of bands, provided a further distraction. It was equally paradoxical that at the time of the movement's gradual emergence later in the decade from the isolation in which it had found itself from those early days – largely through the interest of leading orchestral composers – should coincide with a depression in the movement's fortunes.

Unemployment continued to be the dominant social problem at this time. From one million in 1929, unemployment had risen to 2,500,000 by the end of 1930. The depression grew worse as exports fell and many businesses closed, adding further to the number of unemployed which reached the astronomical figure of three million by 1933. While it was an extremely serious problem in many of the industrial areas, there were other parts of the country that flourished and were relatively unaffected. Here, houses were being built for sale, others were converted to electricity and overall the number of private cars on the roads doubled.

The years of industrial depression in the late 1920s and early 1930s had a mixed effect on the brass band movement. Many accomplished musicians left bands to try and make use of their talents earning a living in theatre orchestras. One of the leading bands of the time, St Hilda's Colliery Band from South Shields, after winning the championship in 1926, were forced to turn professional and toured the country and travelled overseas. Some men on short-time working or wholly unemployed found more leisure in which to practise, but on the other hand many found the sponsorship of employers for a works band withdrawn as they, too, hit hard times. Players from the north moved south in the hope of finding employment in areas less badly affected. This was often a bonus to southern bands and brought infusions of good players or, in some instances, led to new bands coming into existence.

There are many reasons why bands go out of existence, all of which were evidenced further north during this period: social changes, economic difficulties, withdrawal of the all-important support from employers for a works band, and many others. Reading through the records, familiar names of once-famous bands keep recurring. They are in a sense a commentary themselves on social history, their names reflecting industrial and other changes as older industries declined or disappeared to make way for new ones: the change from coal and cloth to aviation and chemicals. It often took little incentive to get a band started. There were usually players available, often with instruments of their own and possessing great faith in their ability, through their music, to raise enough money to keep the band going. This spirit of survival was strong, despite competition from other bands in the same district. Although the following lists may be incomplete, to take a few Yorkshire towns and cities as random examples, there have been at various times at least 35 bands in Hull; a similar number have been supported in Leeds; Sheffield has had at least 29, while not far away Barnsley has seen the same number of bands come and go, many of them famous colliery bands. At different periods Halifax has had 23 bands and Bradford at least 18. Some are still there, a few of them remain at the top of the league. Others have gone, their only recall as nostalgic names in the records.

How fortunes change in the world of banding is well illustrated by the experience of Creswell Colliery Band, a former championship section band, which was forced to wind up its activities in 1978 because of a shortage of players of the required standard and failure to obtain sponsorship. Creswell Colliery Band had been founded in 1899 and reached the top grade during the 1930s and again in the 1950s when it was among the championship bands and a household name through its broadcasts, which numbered around 400. Creswell found that life is tough at the top. To remain there, a band needs to win contests regularly: to win contests a band needs good players and instruments. Replacement of instruments is virtually impossible without the assistance of generous sponsorship and, in the case of colliery and works bands, there is the added problem of support from their employers in time and facilities, if not finance. Among colliery bands, the support of Coal Board local and area officials varies according to the interest of the officials in brass banding. Officials of the Creswell Band at the time of its disbandment complained that they had found the Midlands area of the National Coal Board less generous in their support than the neighbouring Yorkshire area board. Although a junior section band was formed some years earlier, the number of players of high standard was insufficient to fill the gaps that appeared in the senior band.

'We had a few youngsters moving up but you cannot rely solely on them: you are lucky if you get two in a hundred making the top grade,' Mr Lewis Moulsdale, the band secretary, said at the time. By the 1970s the band was struggling and slipping into the vicious circle so well known in the band world: it was unable to attract good new players because it was not on a winning streak in contests – and it was not winning contests because it could not draw in good new players. There was added to this difficulty the matter of finance: the much sought-after sponsorship needed to sustain it eluded the band. In July 1978 it sadly foundered, but its once famous name is kept alive by a junior band, through which, one hopes, it might in the future revive.

Despite the enormous enthusiasm for the National Championship, with audiences of 60,000, brass bands had not taken off in the south as they had in the traditional centres in Yorkshire, Lancashire and the Midlands and Scotland and Wales. A leader writer in *The Times* in 1922, obviously impressed at the large attendances, declared that nobody who moved about London could doubt that the Londoner dearly loved a band – 'and on a brass band he simply dotes'. The writer seems to have made some confusion between military brass bands, since he went on to write enthusiastically about military and bands in Birdcage Walk and performances at the bandstand in nearby St James's Park, most of which were given by military bands. However, the writer found pleasure in the fact that in brass bands 'the appreciative auditor is becoming more and more the active participant. When the Band Festival was founded 22 years ago, no London band figured in the competition. London then boasted no working-men's brass band of a sufficiently high standard. Last Saturday London very properly headed the list of entries by a very handsome margin. It is a sign of health when the devotees of a sport or a diversion are no longer content with passive observance and receptivity but feel the impulse to take a hand in it themselves'.

The fact that a southern band – Luton Red Cross, as it was then known – had come second to the Horwich Railway Mechanics' Institute Band had no doubt also impressed the writer. Luton the following year did even better: they came first. But any Northerner would point out that Luton had been trained by a Yorkshireman (Fred Mortimer) and was conducted by another northerner, William Halliwell.

The writer, however, was right in commenting on a significant sign of the times. The widely held belief that brass bands consisted only of miners and mill hands, incapable of playing anything more musically taxing than a specially arranged selection, was gradually being eroded by two factors: the better music that was being written for them and the decreasing emphasis on their working-class origins as players from a wider range of jobs and professions took an active part in banding.

By the middle of the 1930s it was estimated that what was sometimes described as 'this democratic form of music making' was supporting between 4,000 and 5,000 bands in Great Britain. The movement was beginning to settle down to a period of stability after two unsettled decades as a result of the devastation of the First World War, followed by the years of economic slump. On the organizational side of the movement, many regional brass band associations had been formed to supervise band affairs in their areas, including the organization of contests. A healthy rhythm had been restored to brass band activities after the years of dislocation.

These were the great days of the works and colliery bands, the works bands enjoying the sponsorship of industry and the colliery bands largely supported by social welfare levies on the miners or sometimes subsidized by benevolent colliery owners. There was intense competition to obtain good players and much cynicism among bandsmen in the lesser known bands about the methods of recruitment of players of merit. There were allegations of talent scouts scouring the country for fine brass musicians who, it was claimed, did not necessarily have to be skilled in whatever line of business the firm was engaged in. There were offers of houses held out as additional inducements. Bandmasters denied the allegations, pointing out that bandsmen were workers first and musicians second: otherwise they would be in trouble with the management. There were undoubtedly some fine distinctions drawn: officially a top class soloist could take on part-time orchestral or concert work up to two-thirds of his earnings without losing amateur status.

The quality of musicianship among brass band players was frequently praised by leading orchestral conductors. Sir Henry Wood once aptly described the effect on the rostrum of massed brass bands as 'like being in a whirlwind of sound'. Its soloists were often renowned for their musical ability. Facilities were not always generally available at that time for education in music and the brass bands provided an invaluable recruiting ground for young brass players for the major orchestras. Many brass band soloists, having developed their talents from the instrumental tuition and knowledge of the standard works gained from their brass band experience have gone on to distinguished musical careers in many of the great orchestras. Some bands have had an almost overwhelming display of talent in their ranks. Hanwell Band, for instance, produced players of the calibre and standing of Eric Bravington, who was a founder member of the band at the age of seven and became principal trumpet with the London Philharmonic Orchestra of which he was later managing director, all the time retaining his interest in brass bands as a conductor and adjudicator. Rowland Dyson, who became principal trumpet at Covent Garden, and Stanley Brown, principal trombone with the London Symphony Orchestra, were also products of the same band. Jack Mackintosh, who retired as a professor at Kneller Hall after a career which included principal cornet with the BBC Symphony Orchestra, was also brought up among brass bands, notably the former St Hilda's Colliery Band and the nearby Harton Colliery Band, and a soloist with many others. In addition to Jack Mackintosh, who died in 1979, the Harton Band numbered among its past soloists Tony Thorpe, principal trombone at Covent Garden, Enoch Jackson, principal trumpet with Liverpool Philharmonic Orchestra, Harold Jackson, trumpeter with the London Symphony Orchestra, and Fred Atherton, a former band secretary who was tuba player with the BBC North Region Orchestra and won over 200 medals as a soloist. The orchestral career of Harry Mortimer has been referred to. The above examples are but a few of many. It is now, however, a different situation. Most of the musicians joining the professional ranks of the orchestras are more often the products of colleges of music and are probably less deeply involved in the brass band movement.

Broadcasting had also developed strongly by the 1930s – nine million people held radio licences by then – although this was often regarded as a mixed blessing as far as brass bands were concerned. It was, on the one hand, a distraction to both players and the traditional brass band audience whose musical interests were widened by the variety and content of musical broadcasts. The traditional brass band repertoire of musical selections and marches no longer satisfied some listeners whose musical horizons were extended. On the other hand, brass band broadcasts widened the range of brass bands to an audience of thousands at the turn of a switch. Sir Arthur Bliss, then head of the music department at the BBC, and Dr Denis Wright who was also on the staff and whose own compositions for brass bands were favourites among bandsmen, both saw to it that brass bands were well represented in music broadcasts. Sir Athur later recalled how the brass band movement was making solid progress during the 1930s: how the general level of technical accomplishment was improved and musical horizons widened. When Harry Mortimer was appointed brass and military band adviser to the BBC in 1942 he was able to build on their groundwork, at the same time improving the brass band image by involving some of the famous orchestral conductors with whom he had established friendships in his own orchestral playing days. Under his guidance brass and military band broadcasts averaged ten a week and many successful programmes were introduced: programmes with stirring titles like

'*With Flag Unfurled*', '*Sounding Brass and Voices*' and '*Listen to the Band*'.

Unfortunately, in more recent years the number of nationally networked broadcasts by brass bands has declined and some of the top bands appear to have suffered unfairly in this falling off. There are now a mere four or five networked programmes on which brass bands regularly appear. A survey by the *British Bandsman* based on five networked programmes showed that only three bands during 1978 had broadcast on seven occasions, one had six broadcasts, four had five broadcasts, twelve bands broadcast on four occasions, and ten had taken part in three broadcasts. Quite surprisingly Black Dyke Mills Band, City of Coventry, C.W.S. (Manchester) and Ransome Hoffman Pollard each had only two transmissions and Grimethorpe Colliery Band only one.

Television appearances have provided another source, but these do not make up for the deficiency. In any event, there is much complaint about the sound quality of television performances by brass bands. The introduction of local radio in 1967 has gone some way towards filling the gap and there is hope that more benefit will accrue from the proposed expansion of this newer form of broadcasting. Local radio has been of most service to the lower section bands and has been responsible for offering encouragement to aspiring bands, improving standards and giving the opportunity to broadcast to many bands which would never otherwise have appeared on the air.

The period of consolidation in the 1930s was short-lived. The crisis of 1938 and the outbreak of war the following year again interrupted the progress of the movement. Instruments again went into storage; bands were dissolved as their members enlisted in the Services, leaving behind the veterans and those in reserved occupations to keep bands ticking over. Many bands were reduced to a mere handful of players. Others had to contend with all manner of difficulties to keep going. The City of Coventry Band, which had been formed just before the outbreak of war, in May 1939, had to move their headquarters constantly as three successive bandrooms were destroyed in air raids on that city. Nevertheless, they held all their rehearsals as usual and all their engagements were fulfilled. Northfleet Silver Band, which celebrated its centenary in 1978, had to abandon its activities and put their instruments in storage because their bandroom was taken over to house carrier pigeons for the duration of the war. While some bands were depleted and unable to perform, wartime conditions led to the creation of other bands from the remnants of those left behind or, in some cases, entirely new bands. The Home Guard, like the Volunteers of nearly a century earlier, was created and resulted in the formation of a large number of new bands. There were also new bands associated with the Auxiliary (later the National) Fire Service. The present Portsmouth City Band came into existence in this way, and another band, started by auxiliary firemen at Bexley in Kent in 1940, two years later became the official National Fire Service Band in London and, after the war, continued as the North Kent Silver Band.

More than one depleted or dormant band loaned its instruments to one of the new wartime bands. This happened in the case of the West London Silver Band, which had been formed in 1937. During the war it loaned its instruments to the Home Guard, and in 1946 was re-formed as the Borough of Barnes Brass Band. In 1959 it was taken over by Watneys, the brewery nearby. One of its best known members at one time was the comedian Jimmy Edwards, who played the tenor horn with the band.

The peak of wartime mobilization had been reached in 1943 when 22 million men and women out of a total adult population available for service of 33 million were in the Forces, Civil Defence or employed in essential industry. Conscription had been extended to the age of 41. By the time the war ended 400,000 people had been killed, 60,000 of them civilians killed in air raids. The final toll, while considerably fewer than the 750,000 dead in the First World War, was nevertheless heavy. Brass bands again suffered no less than other groups

Coal mines have provided as rich a source for brass bands as have other industrial activities: many of the finest bands have emerged from small colliery communities, despite the obvious difficulties arising from the shift system with rehearsals and engagements. Many of them received benevolent support from generous colliery owners in pre-nationalization days, while in other cases levies of modest sums – often as little as a few pence per week per head – from every miner at a colliery have helped to swell the band funds and provide new instruments or uniforms.

The ups and downs of the coal industry have made for a fairly high casualty rate among colliery bands but they remain a strong force in the movement, fielding over 50 bands at their own annual contest in Blackpool, and there are usually four or five colliery bands represented in the championships at Belle Vue and the championship section of the national finals in London.

There are often strong links between the colliers and Salvation Army bands. It was local miners in 1879 who helped to form the

Salvation Army's first corps band at Consett, Co. Durham. Colliery bands were among the earliest bands to be formed. Their particular strength is in their unity, coming as they do from close-knit communities.

The coal mining industry had faced countless problems between the wars and, indeed, during the Second World War when many young miners left to join the Forces in order to escape going down the pits. The average age of miners was increasing and output was falling. By the end of the war it was an industry that could no longer pay its way and was, therefore, ripe for nationalization when the post-war Labour Government came to power. The Coal Mines Act of 1946 took coal mines out of private ownership and set up the National Coal Board to run them.

The future of the many colliery bands under the new set-up was something which gave rise to much concern at the time. Many of the private colliery owners had supported their bands: musical miners had moved from one colliery to another where there was a better band. Would a bureaucratic organization like the new Coal Board continue to sponsor and support the bands? Colliery bands had, in most cases, managed to continue during the war and apart from the material contribution of miners generally to the war effort, the bands had helped keep up morale with their concerts and broadcasts. But with shortages of staff and all the other wartime problems it had not been easy and gaps had been filled by the use of female players, the wives and daughters of miners, and young players.

Under private ownership there had been a welfare organization supported by levies on the industry. Under the new arrangements, the Coal Industry Social Welfare Organization was set up with colliery brass bands as one of its responsibilities. The organization has assisted bands with grants for the replacement of instruments and in Yorkshire, which has a high proportion of colliery bands, operates an instrument pool to which older instruments when they are replaced are despatched to be re-issued to learners and juniors. The CISWO also organizes the annual miners' band festival, which is held at Blackpool.

In recent years an increasing number of conductors has emerged from the ranks of players and the Coal Industry Social Welfare Organization in 1979 announced the inauguration of a scholarship, named after Sir Derek Ezra, chairman of the Coal Board, and run in conjunction with the Royal Academy of Music, providing a two-year course in brass band conducting open to bandsmen working in the mines or to the sons and daughters of miners.

Nationalization of the mines and the consequent reduction of the work force as a result of rationalization has brought about some dilution in the qualifications for colliery bands. Many bands have had to fill gaps by taking on players from outside the collieries or opening up membership of bands to sons and daughters of mining employees. The rules have been relaxed nowadays to the extent that only half the number of players in the band must either work in the colliery or be the sons or daughters of working miners or colliery officials.

Like their counterparts in the famous Welsh choirs, miners have a deep love of music. A writer in *Coal Quarterly*, a publication of the National Coal Board, in 1964 referred to some of the misconceptions that were held about colliery bandsmen. They were, he wrote, 'not a bunch of beefy, red-faced men in uncomfortable, ill-fitting uniforms with beer bottles protruding from their pockets but smartly dressed, well-disciplined groups of men, proud of their place in pit village life and with a dedicated love of music. They worry about the condition of their lips as chorus girls worry about their legs'.

Colliery bands were, perhaps surprisingly, among the first to admit women players into their ranks. Initially it was to fill vacancies created by the war, but the practice has since been extended. Women had played a prominent part in the Salvation Army sphere of brass bands for many years before they began to make their appearance in secular bands. The distinction of being the first woman to play a brass instrument in an Army band goes to Mrs Davey, wife of Captain Abram Davey, commanding officer of Portsmouth Salvation Army who publicized her wish to obtain a cornet in the columns of *The War Cry*, the Army's weekly newspaper, as far back as 1880. When he was succeeded by Captain Valentine Case in October of the same year, Case also set about forming a band. He had been an accomplished musician before entering the Salvation Army and with his two daughters and himself on brass instruments and his wife playing the cymbals, they formed the nucleus of the Portsmouth band. As will be referred to later, a Salvation Army women's band was formed in Australia in 1905 and there was a Lassies' Band in New Zealand.

In the case of competing bands, the pioneering women players invariably came from a family background of established brass band players. Their entry was fairly undramatic: a gradual infiltration which roughly coincided with the outbreak of the Second World War. They were then few in number: it was not until after the war that women joined bands in any number. By the 1950s, however, at least one colliery band had seven girls among its complement.

There were at any rate four girls competing in a national solo contest in 1938. One of them was a 13-year-old girl cornet player, Grace Cole, who was then a member of the Firbeck Colliery Band, near Rotherham, the only colliery band at that time featuring a girl player. Her father, a colliery deputy, played in the same band and seven of her relations were also brass bandsmen. After leaving school she worked in the offices of Manvers Main Colliery, thus qualifying to play in that colliery band. By this time she was earning a reputation as an accomplished solo player and in 1942 she won an Alexander Owen scholarship, being the first girl to compete and the only girl to win a scholarship. Dr Denis Wright, who founded the National Youth Brass Band, composed a cornet solo, *La Mantella*, which he dedicated to her. During the war she attained a national reputation through her solo appearances with leading bands such as Besses o' th' Barn and Grimethorpe Colliery Band and many others, and through broadcasts. After the war she left the amateur brass band scene and formed an all-female band in which she played the trumpet. She has more recently returned to amateur playing, after bringing up her family, as a member of Croydon Borough Band.

Another of the competitors in that 1938 contest was tenor horn player, Betty Anderson, who is now conductor of Ratby (Leicestershire) Band, with which in 1978 she made her place in brass band history by becoming the first woman to conduct at the Belle Vue Championships. She is also an adjudicator and chairman of the National Youth Brass Band. She comes from a banding family with a history in the movement going back over 100 years. Her grandfather played in one of the last of the town waits in Leicester, while her father was also a bandsman in the same band with which Betty Anderson started her banding career, Leicester Imperial, which she joined at the age of eight. All played the tenor horn.

'We always had instruments about the house and I do not recall a time when brass bands were not talked about,' she recalls. 'We had them at breakfast, dinner and tea. When I first joined the band in 1938 I was amongst the first three or four girls in the country to do so. It did not occur to me at that time that girls did not play in brass bands. I thought everybody did. I began to take part in solo competitions all over the country and often I got the comment "Well done, my boy" from the adjudicator when I got my marks, so unusual was it for a girl competitor.' Alongside her

Miss Betty Anderson rehearsing with the Ratby Band.

(Photo by courtesy of *The Times*)

increasingly successful Ratby Band, Betty Anderson now runs a junior band and learners' classes, but in her own early days in the movement there were no such facilities. 'There was no instruction as such in those days,' she says. 'If the man next to you told you which half of the page of music you were on, you were lucky. I was grateful to the people who sat by me.'

Betty Anderson's father taught and encouraged her. He, too, was a successful soloist and together they did the rounds of the solo competitions, sharing the same instrument. She entered her first competition only five weeks after taking up playing the horn. She won 2s. 6d. (12½p) in fourth place in the under-16 class, playing *Sweet and Low*. In 1944 she made her first broadcast in a programme devised by Harry Mortimer for young brass musicians and she also played solo at concerts accompanied by some of the leading bands like Black Dyke Mills and Fodens – an experience she describes as being 'the equivalent of a young footballer being invited to play for Manchester United at Wembley'. She began her conducting career when she was a mere 14 years old with a local Air Training Corps band run by her father. At 18 she became deputy bandmaster of the Leicester Imperial Band, which had come into existence in the early 1900s at a period when there were more than ten bands in the Leicester area. She remained with that band for 25 years, the last six as conductor, then moved to nearby Kibworth Band, with whom she played for ten years and competed with them at the Royal Albert Hall national championships. Then came the break with Kibworth and her appointment as conductor of Ratby Band, with whom she has had almost astronomical success.

Betty Anderson says she cannot understand why girls were such late starters in the brass band movement. 'Probably it was because parents thought the environment was not right for girls,' she says. 'The players were generally older men. There was nobody in the band at that time under their mid-thirties. Then there was the fact that bands usually met for practice in a public house. But I have had tremendous encouragement and have never met with any prejudice because I was a woman. If a player happened to swear, he would always apologise to me. When I moved to Kibworth Band I was playing for the first time with people of my own age group. That was really the first time I had been a woman in a man's world: before that I had been a girl in an old man's world. There were no other women in the band at that time. I realized I was the exception and I did not want them to change their ways for my benefit. I told them: "Don't worry about not saying things. What I don't want to hear I will not hear." I was always willing to make my own acceptable rules. But, having said that, during my entire banding career I have never been in any group of bandsmen who have made me think I would not want my mother or my grandmother hearing their conversation. From a woman's point of view I have been particularly lucky.'

Miss Anderson admits to some concern about the public image of bandsmen and drinking. 'Bandsmen do drink, but then so do Rugby players and choral singers,' she says. Her own father was a teetotaller but that did not prevent him from taking part in banding. When the band held their practices in a room over a public house he, accompanied by his daughter, would enter the premises by a back door.

It is perhaps inevitable that in a small community like Ratby a woman conductor becomes more involved than a male counterpart in some of the personal problems of her players, some of which may have a bearing on a player's performance. Banding itself has an important social function in this respect; it often helps as an antidote to all manner of problems. Some cynics, of course, might argue conversely that it can also create a few problems. But talking to Betty Anderson one soon realizes that she regards her involvement in helping to sort out problems as an important part of her duties, along with the musical training and conducting.

Barbara Stone, despite her comparative youth, is another pioneer in the increasing role of women in the brass band movement. To her goes the distinction of being the first woman to conduct a band in the championship section at the Albert Hall contests. She, too, comes from a family steeped in brass banding: one uncle was conductor and another uncle a player in the brass band in her native Dorchester, Dorset. Through their involvement she determined at a very early age to be a musician. She started to play the piano at the age of five and two years later was taught the cornet by her musical uncles, playing with them in the band. At 14 she played with the National Youth Brass Band, in which she was deputy principal to Philip McCann, now a distinguished member and soloist with Black Dyke Mills Band. At 18, Barbara Stone went to the Royal Academy of Music to study the piano and, under William Overton, who had a strong Salvationist background, the trumpet. While at the academy she became a playing member of the Hanwell Band (now known as Roneo Vickers Band) from 1963 to 1970, during which time she became deputy conductor to Eric Bravington. She left in 1971 to become conductor of the British Rail Band at Swindon; during this period the band competed in the Albert Hall finals for the first time in its history and was placed ninth. In 1977 she returned to the Hanwell Band as musical director and left them to freelance as conductor and adjudicator in 1979. She is now a music teacher at a school in Hertfordshire.

As a young girl player, the only one in the band, she says she was not a spectacle but an object of attention. Like her predecessors her own involvement was based on a mixture of family background in the movement and her own determination. More recently, however, greater opportunities have arisen for girls – and young people in general – to develop an interest in brass bands, both through school and through parental encouragement. 'If women are going to take any part in this movement they should do it because they have an ability and not for any other reason. Most women want to be taken seriously for their ability', says Mrs Stone.

Had she met with any prejudices? 'I have managed to cast them aside in that I have been accepted for what I had to offer. It is a tough world and the only way I could have survived is in that way,' she replied. 'Bands are after success and are only interested in something that will help to bring them that success. It has to be harder for a woman but prejudice against women has never been a problem as far as I am concerned. It is not the same everywhere, though. I believe there are still places where the women have to travel in a different coach, for instance.

'Men cannot freely use the same language in front of women or tell the same jokes. Women should be prepared to accept whatever that means: they should learn to listen to the jokes. You cannot expect to go into a predominantly male scene and try to change it . . . If women are in it [banding] for the right reasons there is nothing that men can object to . . . It is said sometimes that women have not got the sustaining power but they have proved that they have and women have proved themselves to be just as dedicated as men, so I do not know why some bands do not accept them.'

Mrs Stone believes that women are more readily accepted among the lower section bands, but she has no doubt about the direction of her own future career. 'Championship banding is where I want to stay,' she says. 'And having achieved some success myself in this area I hope that others will follow.' She also has no doubts about the increasing numbers of women who will take part in the movement as players and conductors. 'Many more girls are learning to play brass instruments now in schools. They are going to take their place in the National Youth Brass Band and in other bands. A much greater proportion of women are going to take a serious interest in banding in the future,' she predicts.

Other women conductors include Mrs Bessie Ackroyd, who conducts Harry Mortimer's old band, Hebden Bridge; Joyce Morgan, conductor of Abertillery; and Julie Holling, musical director of Maltby Miners' Band, to name but three. As regards players, it is estimated that of the 3,000 or so musicians taking part in the annual National Championships, ten per cent are girls aged between eight and twenty. Some bands have only one female player, while others have a higher proportion. The largest number in one band is the Kilmarnock Concert Brass, the 1979 Scottish champions, which, in 1979, had 17 girls among its players.

Another interesting development in the brass band movement in recent years is the extension of sponsorship by commercial firms. There is a long tradition of sponsorship from the earliest days of bands being supported by the owner of a works or a colliery. But sponsorship has grown into big business and many more bands, previously supported by the small subscriptions of members but now feeling the harsh effects of inflation and the heavy costs of replacing instruments, are joining in the search for commercial patronage. It can be a mortifying experience for a band when those who encouraged it to come together, be it a local firm or a local community, fails to sustain its interest. In the case of a community which once provided a band with many opportunities to perform at regular processions of local organizations, at Sunday school outings or fêtes, and particularly the park bandstand, social and economic changes have changed the habits of the public, who now look elsewhere for their entertainment.

THE NEW BANDSTAND. SOUTHEND-ON-SEA.

Brass Bands were an outdoor form of entertainment. This ornate bandstand at Southend-on-Sea, built in the early 1900s, is typical of the architectural excesses of the period. The movable screens protected the bandsmen from the strong sea breezes.

One of the traditional platforms for brass bands, the park or promenade bandstand on a Sunday afternoon, has almost disappeared in most towns and cities. Bandstands, themselves often objects of considerable architectural interest, have been demolished, dismantled or vandalized. It is paradoxical that at a time when there is increasing public interest in brass bands this traditional platform has virtually disappeared. Cutbacks in local authority spending as a result of the country's economic situation in recent years has had a disastrous effect on such concerts. In London, the budgetary reductions of the entertainments section of the Greater London Council's parks department has resulted in the concert season being reduced in duration, together with a reduction in the number of concert venues. Where outdoor concerts are still held, there is often controversy over fees. Because of the cutbacks in expenditure some local authorities no longer pay bands a fee, but instead allow them to play and take a collection among the audience to cover their travel and other expenses. This is not always a popular arrangement: some bands refuse to accept such terms, arguing that they could easily meet with a loss.

Even more disastrous to a band can be the withdrawal of financial support from a sponsor who, from motives of either benevolence or prestige, encouraged a works band but as frequently happened some years ago found more urgent needs for its expenditure. There was a noticeable flagging of interest on the part of some sections of industry during the 1950s. Firms were usually frank about the reasons. The company responsible for the Clayton Aniline Works Band, for example, announcing the demise of that formerly well-known band, stated: 'The company has decided with regret to discontinue the works band as it is becoming increasingly difficult to maintain a first-class band at a reasonable cost and also to recruit bandsmen of necessary musical qualification who fulfil the company's requirements for the other work they have to perform.' Changes in management have also frequently resulted in disbandment when incoming executives without an interest in banding have been less responsive to the facilities and costs required.

By the 1970s, however, take-overs in the brass band world increased almost as much as industrial take-overs, although the financial gains were less comparable. There is certainly little money to be made from taking over a band, indeed the reverse, but the rapid growth of musical patronage indicates that there are indirect benefits, notably in terms of prestige.

The amounts involved in sponsorship are variable, from a few hundred pounds to several thousand for the provision of instruments and uniforms; accommodation for band practices, and band's expenses while travelling. There are endless examples of take-overs by industry where rising costs have borne down excessively on previously unsupported bands: in the north-east the former Craghead Colliery Band re-emerged as the Ever Ready Band, supported by the well-known battery company; in the Potteries the Royal Doulton Band arose from the remains of the

North Staffordshire Concert Band; when Blackpool Town Band felt the financial pinch an engineering firm came to the rescue and it emerged as the Dutton-Forshaw Motors Band; in Greater Manchester when Kearsley Band fell on hard times it was given an injection and became the works band of the American-owned Eaton Transmission Gear Group; Wakefield Youth Band accepted sponsorship by the Sirdar wool company in 1975; the former Rockingham Colliery Band was taken over in 1978 by an engineering concern to become the Osborne Rockingham Band; Clipstone Colliery Welfare Band is now sponsored by Torque Tension Ltd who manufacture equipment for the mining industry.

The agricultural section of Albright & Wilson took over in 1978 sponsorship of the 100-year-old Brigg Band in Lincolnshire, which incidentally plays entirely for pleasure and now has new instruments and sports new uniforms in the company's colours; the former Hanwell Band, for 88 years a subscription band, was taken over in 1979 by the Roneo Vickers office equipment group and changed its name accordingly; Cambridge Band is sponsored by the Co-operative Movement (the movement sponsors a number of bands and is fairly blatant about its investment: out of the 22 bands in the 1979 Belle Vue contest, the C.W.S. (Manchester) Band was the only one to advertise openly with the familiar Co-op emblem prominently emblazoned on the bass drum). The Norwest Co-op support New Mills Band, one of the oldest surviving bands, by allowing them to use premises as a bandroom; the City of Birmingham Band changed its name to City of Birmingham Delta Band when a West Bromwich metals company chipped in with £1,000 towards providing a regular musical director, replacing instruments and buying new uniforms; Lockwood Band, formed after the Second World War from the remnants of a Home Guard band, while not becoming a works band, added to their title the name of a local firm, Joseph Lumb & Sons Ltd, in whose premises they have rehearsed for 30 years.

Sponsorship does not always follow the familiar form of support for a particular band. In the last few years, contest sponsorship by commercial firms has become almost as popular as the financial backing for a works band. Butlins and Pontins, two leaders of the holiday camp business, have both extended their interest in brass bands by sponsoring youth and other band contests; Rothman cigarettes, Vaux Breweries in the north-east and Lansing Bagnall, manufacturers of fork-lift equipment are among major commercial companies now sponsoring contests, while others are run by local authorities sometimes in association with a local firm. In 1979 the Britvic soft drinks firm helped with the sponsorship of the Mineworkers' annual contest.

The benefits of sponsorship are often intangible, but there is evidence that a works band is worth the investment in return for the advertisement it affords in promoting sales, particularly in the case of firms producing consumer products. It is probably the cheapest form of advertising. Geoffrey Whitham, musical director of Hammonds Sauce Works Band, estimated that when his band was named BBC Band of the Year some time ago his group's sales increased by the astonishing figure of 25 per cent.

Cynics would say that some bands in the championship section have travelled dangerously near the dividing line between amateur and professional status. One band that did turn professional, St Hilda's Colliery Band from South Shields, which was at the time enjoying a highly successful run of championship victories, was forced into it by circumstances of the time. Its run of victories in contests resulted in the inevitable flood of invitations to perform at concerts all over the country. St Hilda's were criticized for accepting an unlimited number of invitations, with the conse-quential effect on their finances, and incurred a stern warning from the organizer of the National Championships that this was contrary to the spirit of amateur status. From the proceeds of these engagements St Hilda's paid within a year for their own well-equipped coach in which to travel to their engagements – a piece of economic foresight which not only brought them a cor-responding saving in transport costs but, in view of future devel-opments, turned out to be a wise investment. The initial warning was ignored and the following year when the colliery closed dur-ing the period of depression in the coal industry the entire band became dependent for their income on their engagement fees and prize money.

Their victory in the National Championship of 1926 brought matters to a head. They were barred from competing the following year and, while still able to sport their 'champion band' label but dropping 'colliery' from their title because of its potential damage to their image in the industrial climate of the period, turned professional. They carried on successfully for a decade until a falling-off of profitable engagements coupled with the ill-health of their extremely capable manager, James Southern, who had acted in that capacity for 27 years, brought about the demise of the band after their final engagement at an agricultural show in Sep-tember 1937.

The line between amateur and professional can be seen to be

a fine one indeed. It is one on which in recent years the Musicians' Union has cast a watchful eye and some heated exchanges have ensued. It is a distinction much more finely drawn than is the case with other amateur musical groups such as choral societies and amateur operatic companies.

Many of the top championship bands are able to claim large sums for their concert appearances: ironically, these concers are often arranged by small local bands to raise money for their own funds. It is estimated that on winning the National Championship a band can immediately add £100 to its concert appearance fee.

Versatility is one of the outstanding attributes of brass bandsmen and while some of the contemporary or *avant-garde* music of recent years has broken down barriers in the more controversial branches of music, brass bands have also been gaining in popularity at the other end of the spectrum in the pop music section.

The various idioms have been brought together in both concert programmes and on records. Black Dyke Mills Band have fused their inimitable sound with the music of ex-Beatle Paul McCartney. Tunes with a Latin American beat giving full rein to percussionists have proved to be popular items. In 1972 a young jazz pianist and singer, Peter Skellern, chose the Hanwell Band to provide backing for his recording of *You're a lady*, which entered the popular music charts. It is a practice he has developed, latterly using the Grimethorpe Colliery Band for backing and their appearances on television in the BBC Best of Brass programmes have attracted much comment, not all of it favourable. Another contribution in this field was that of the youthful Tintwhistle Band who played the accompaniment for Bryan and Michael for a record entitled *Matchstalk Men*, a musical tribute to the Lancashire artist, L.S. Lowry.

One of the greatest boosts to the brass band sphere in recent years, however, was the recording by the Brighouse and Rastrick Band in 1977 of their conductor, Derek Broadbent's arrangement of the Cornish air *The Floral Dance*. It was an immediate if unexpected success and rapidly rose in the Top Ten, only a record by Paul McCartney preventing it from reaching the top position. The immediate results were an immense general upsurge of interest in brass bands, and heated controversy and criticism from the purists. The band was feted at civic receptions, its members were interviewed by journalists, and television crews descended to film them. Their engagement book swelled: in the year following their success they attended 44 engagements as well as charity performances and three contest appearances. Their success put the band on a sound financial basis. They already owned their own head-quarters, complete with concert hall, in Brighouse. One year's royalties alone, excluding later overseas royalties, brought them in £50,000, which is being used to further the band's objective of encouraging the growth of brass band music. The members of the band have donated ten cornets to five schools in the district, and some of the money has also been used to buy land at the rear of their headquarters for a larger car park, to renovate their head-quarters and to replace instruments.

They have faced criticism from some of their own members for neglecting the contest field of their activities, particularly when they withdrew from the 1978 championships. Band officials ex-plained that the withdrawal was not a question of them not being concerned about contests any more but because their commit-ments prevented them from rehearsing the test-piece to competi-tion standard. Perfection is their goal and this they demonstrated in the 1978 British Open championship with their first win for 48 years by scoring two points more than Black Dyke Band and denying their neighbours and rivals a double hat-trick. The test-piece, the overture *Benvenuto Cellini* by Berlioz, was a far cry from their 'pop' chart success and demonstrated their versatility to any doubters.

The record sales were evidence of the popularity of the Brig-house sound among people not normally associated with brass bands. But within the movement the Brighouse success sparked off a long argument over the place and image of the modern brass band. There were the purists of the movement who held it was not the role of the brass band to entertain, that the playing of entertaining pieces would lower standards of performance; and that they should not be imitating the music and style of pop groups.

'The name of our game is music, not the entertainment of the general public,' one correspondent wrote angrily if somewhat shortsightedly to *The British Bandsman*. He went on to argue that the brass band was a legitimate art form and for that reason would, like the orchestra, never become a popular form of enter-tainment. The brass band, he wrote, should be recognized as a serious musical activity; only in that way would it receive the appreciation it deserved.

That was the minority view of the hard-line traditionalist, of whom there are many, let it be said. The majority, though, sup-ported the view that Derek Broadbent himself put forward, that they had attempted to reach – and succeeded – a vast new audience of people who would not normally listen to brass bands and, in doing so, other brass bands would eventually benefit. No concert programme is likely to suit every listener in its entirety. The conductor who did would have worked a miracle. In formulating a concert programme, band officials have to bear in mind the tastes of their customers, the audience. That entertaining music is wanted there is no doubt. Organizers have to remember that the object is to entertain the audience whatever its varied tastes; they have, therefore, to steer a careful middle course of mixing traditional, popular and contemporary music.

Much the same problem faces the organizers of the national brass band festival each year, where the programme content invariably provokes criticism. It must be tempting for the organizers to retreat to the comparative safety of the *status quo*, but such an occasion demands a responsibility which, one must add, has not been shirked, to help extend the movement's horizons by keeping audiences abreast of new musical trends. Whatever some of the purists in the movement may argue, 10,000 people go to the Royal Albert Hall festival each year to be entertained.

The National Championships in the Royal Albert Hall. The honour for which all bands strive, the National Championship Challenge Trophy, occupies pride of place.

(Photo by courtesy of *The Times*)

While the Brighouse record was a money-spinner, brass band records in general, despite their profusion and often high quality, have rarely met with an overwhelming or even satisfactory response from retailers. Too often they are hidden away in a miscellaneous section or mixed up with the records of military bands. Brass band recordings have become victims of a vicious circle in record retailing which started when large department stores began selling records and, because of the quantities involved, offering large discounts on popular albums. Smaller independent retailers found it difficult to compete and sought to make up their profits by stocking popular, quick selling records, a category which did not include brass band recordings. At the same time some of the major recording companies dropped brass band records from their titles. It has been left to small record producers and specialist retailers to fill the gap.

Records have nevertheless proved a modestly profitable way of raising funds and there has been a marked increase in recent years in the number of lower section bands and youth and school bands making records.

A further important influence in the growing interest in brass bands in the last two decades has been the development of school and youth bands, in which the competitive element is as strong as in the senior bands and which are now catered for with their own contests. Eight is said to be the ideal age for learning to play a brass instrument; certainly an encouragement to children in learning a brass instrument is the fact, discovered by worker players over 150 years ago, that they are easier to play and produce quicker results than most other instruments. Instrument rental schemes operated by manufacturers have alo proved an advantage as costs of new instruments have soared. Such schemes have meant that parental money has not been wasted if a young player becomes disinterested after a time.

Many local authorities have encouraged the growth of brass bands in schools and assistance is forthcoming in this respect from the National School Brass Band Association, which was formed in 1953. It then had 20 bands in membership; there are now around 250. Two other national organizations have also been invaluable in their encouragement and training of young brass players: the National Youth Brass Band, formed in 1951 by the late Dr Denis Wright, and the National Youth Brass Band of Scotland, which was formed in 1958. The latter, while operating on similar lines to its English counterpart, performs only original works and has been responsible for commissioning a growing list of brass band compositions, making a valuable addition to the repertoire.

What happens when enthusiastic young players leave school? There is now an acute awareness of the potential pool of players produced in schools, and many of the leading bands have formed junior bands to retain the interest of young players and to provide a reservoir of players to fill recurring gaps in the main bands.

Encouragement in schools is not, of course, nation-wide. Miss Betty Anderson, chairman of the National Youth Band, for instance, comments: 'unfortunately some of the people in charge in the schools are sometimes twenty years or more behind in their thinking. They still frown on brass bands.'

The Ratby Band from Leicestershire, of which Betty Anderson is musical director, provides a typical example of the grassroots of brass banding and the changes of the last few years. Ratby is a fairly isolated village in what was once a colliery area. The road through Ratby does not lead anywhere: you have to have a reason for going to the village. 'It is like a bit of Yorkshire dropped into Leicestershire: it is so unlike the rest of the country. Even the dialect they speak is quite different from the rest of Leicestershire.' says Miss Anderson. Ratby Band is a small village band with a history as exciting as any of the championship bands. It was formed over 70 years ago and spent 68 of them in the fourth or lowest section. But in seven years it has advanced from the fourth to the championship section, won the Grand Shield Section at Belle Vue in 1978; competed in the British Open championship, and won the World Championship in the Second Section in Holland in 1978. The band was promoted to the championship section in January 1979.

When Betty Anderson arrived as conductor seven years ago the band was under strength. Now, from a village of 2,900 inhabitants there are more than 80 players living within five miles of the bandroom; there is a junior band and a learner's class. Would-be new members arrive each week: brothers and sisters of existing young players wait to join as soon as they are old enough. Behind the band is a group of about 30 non-players and tremendous enthusiasm from a large group of parents.

'We grow our own players here,' says Miss Anderson. 'My ambition was to conduct the band at Belle Vue. I achieved that. My next ambition is to conduct the band there again – and win. As I conducted them at Belle Vue I felt particularly proud as I recalled that I had seen ten of the players in the band that day put an instrument to their lips for the first time.'

All the money to support the band comes from the villagers in the form of the proceeds of jumble sales and raffles, etc. – and from an annual concert which has been held for the past six years in a local hall which is always filled to its 600 capacity without any major form of advertising. Whenever the band has an engagement the villagers are there to support it. Other organizations check the engagement book because it is pointless to organize anything else in the village when the band is in action.

Betty Anderson says of her band's success: 'I got to the right group of people at the right time and we just flew off from there. It was quite astronomical. The smallness of the community 'helps. Parents involve themselves in all sorts of ways to help the band. People have actually changed their jobs because their work interfered with rehearsals. People who have left the village come back to support us. What worries me though is that the supporting money for the band is coming all the time from the same people. In the case of young players schemes for the hire of instruments are helpful. But how could we find £7,000 for four new basses? We must eventually seek for sponsorship.'

Ratby Band, like many others, has close links with bands in Holland, with which there are frequent exchange visits. It is interchange of this nature and visits by leading figures of the British brass band movement that has led to the growth in Europe in recent years of British-style brass bands.

Visits by well-known British bands – Black Dyke Mills Band, for instance, visited Germany in 1978 and Norway in 1979 on tours sponsored by Boosey & Hawkes, the British firm of instrument manufacturers – have also done much to impress European bandsmen and convert them to the British-style band and useful contacts have been made during visits by foreign bandsmen to the various British contests. Dutch bands were not all-brass in prewar days but since the end of the war, encouraged by contacts with British bands, there has been an increase in the number of bands organized on the lines of British bands in Holland, which now stages its own annual championships. A pioneer in this conversion was Pieter Jan Molenaar (he died in 1979) who also built up one of the largest European brass and military band music publishing houses. In Denmark, the Concord Band formed in 1957 from members of the Danish Boys' Brigade marked the introduction of British style bands to that country where in the region of 28 bands now compete in National Championships. A Federation of Belgian Brass Bands was formed in 1978 while close links have been established between Great Britain and bands in

Norway, Switzerland and Sweden, whose Solna Brass has made several successful visits to Britain.

Unlike Britain, most overseas countries have established national organizations to co-ordinate banding activities throughout their countries. All efforts to effect a national organization in this country, however, have so far defied realization. It is the dream of men such as Harry Mortimer that eventually some such central organization will come into existence. Several efforts have been made, particularly at the time of the retirement of Edwin Vaughan Morris, to establish some kind of central body to coordinate all the banding activities. The fact that when men such as Enderby Jackson, Henry Iles and Edwin Vaughan Morris were the dominant characters of the movement meant that they were effectively the national organization and the need for anything else was superfluous. The need for such an organization now is becoming more urgent as expansion goes on apace. It is to be hoped the movement realizes and meets the need before it is too late.

Chapter Five

'Blowing troubadors of God'

No study of the brass band movement can afford to ignore the important role of Salvation Army bands. Like town and works bands, 'Army' bands stem from the old church and evangelical bands and are very much a part of the brass band scene today. The Salvation Army bands in a sense are a movement within the main movement, although there are strict conditions laid down and adhered to which prevent them playing music other than that which is specially composed for them and, of course, they are not permitted to engage in competitive musical activities. But their public performances and concerts bring them within the ambit of the brass band movement. There are other reasons for including them: a spell with a Salvation Army band has been the starting point for many a successful brass bandsman and, despite the rigidity of the Army rules, there is considerable interchange between the two types of band. Many players from Salvationist bands find a welcome place in a secular band when they leave the Salvation Army; and there is often an exchange in the reverse direction. Secular bands frequently are invited to give concerts at Salvation Army centres and some of the composers of the Salvation Army's sacred music have also composed for competitive bands, as the Army musicians call their secular colleagues. The outstanding example in recent years is Eric Ball, a prolific composer of music for both idioms since the Second World War. The bandsmens' newspapers are copious in their coverage of the affairs of Salvation Army bands both in Britain and throughout the world and bandsmen generally have great respect for the musical abilities of the Army musicians. There is, therefore, a close affinity between the two types of brass band.

The Army bands vary from the prestigious International Staff Band and highly accomplished bands in other countries and at

some of the larger citadels in Britain, to the vast conglomeration
of musical groups varying in ability and performance in corps
throughout the world. The widely accepted image of the average
Salvation Army band as a small group of musicians blowing an
accompaniment to the hymns beneath the light of a street lamp
is an impression that does them an injustice. It takes no account
of the professional way in which they are organized or the dedication of the bandsmen and their role both as music-makers
combining militant Christianity with their music and as musical
ambassadors, teaching the intricacies of playing brass instruments
or evoking an interest in music among the inhabitants of often
primitive places all over the world who might otherwise never
have heard of brass bands.

General William Booth, founder of the Salvation Army, equated
the rallying beat of the big bass drum with the church bell. Considering the historic association between bands and religion expressed in the old church bands, it is not surprising that music
should from an early stage have had such an important part in
the strident evangelism of the Salvation Army. These musical
missioners have been 'blowing salvation down every street', as
one of their officers once said, for more than 100 years; the
centenary of Army bands was celebrated in July, 1978 at a colossal
world congress in London.

Many 'outside' brass bands were already well established before
their introduction to the Salvation Army. Initially they were regarded by the founder as 'a little novelty' and cautiously accepted
by him. After a visit to the north of England in August 1877 he
reported that: 'the last Sabbath we had a little novelty which
apparently worked well. Among the converts were two members
of a brass band. One plays a cornet and to utilise him at once he
was put with his cornet in the front rank of the procession from
South Stockton. He certainly improved the singing and brought
crowds all along the line of the march.'

These early Christian Missioners, as they were originally called,
frequently met with prejudice and persecution, expressed not only
verbally but physically as they pronounced their religious message
and sought converts in market squares and other public places.
The addition of the big bass drum and other instruments to draw
attention to their outdoor activities was often regarded as a dis-
turbance of the peace. These pioneering bandsmen were described
as hooligans using religion as a cloak in order to disturb the
peaceful atmosphere.

The use of individual instrumentalists to augment the singing or to draw attention to the evangelists had been observed in a number of places but it was physical violence against a group of pioneer missioners in Salisbury that led to the formation of the first Salvation Army band. The evangelists had made their appearance in the Wiltshire town in March 1878 and disturbed the quiet with their singing and preaching in the market place seeking converts before marching to a former joinery shop which they used as their mission hall.

Charles Fry was a master builder who had played the cornet in the band of the local Volunteers, as had so many other early bandsmen, and taught his three sons to play brass instruments. Their appearance with the missioners was a brave response to the need for protection for the evangelists: a musical bodyguard against attack. In doing so they laid the foundations for what has developed into an important addition to the Salvationists' Christian service and a significant part in religious music. Charles Fry thus became the Salvation Army's first Bandmaster: the band, composed of him and his three sons, consisted of two cornets, a valve trombone and a euphonium. They were no strangers to religious music or to preaching. Charles Fry, a respected lay preacher in the town, had led the chapel orchestra and choir and had organized concerts of sacred music; his eldest son Fred had played second cornet in the orchestra at the age of eight and had become organist when the orchestra was disbanded.

Reports on the successful musical support of the 'hallelujah brass band' at Salisbury and elsewhere in the West Country were made to William Booth who paid a visit there to see for himself. While realizing the potential of such music as an adjunct of his missioners' soul-saving endeavours, Booth was a cautious man. As a trial he invited Fry and his family to accompany him on several of his campaigns about the country. Fry found it difficult with all the travelling to maintain his building business. In May 1880 the business was sold and the family left Salibsury for London to form the nucleus of the first 'staff band' of the Salvation Army.

The big bass drum, which was to become a symbol of vigorous evangelism and Salvation Army bands, was added to the Fry family's band in 1879 – a large, curiously shaped model that was suspended from the ceiling and could be used only indoors. It was later altered in size and shape to enable its use on parades and at outdoor meetings, but the citizens of Salisbury would permit its use for some time on Sundays only. Fry's musical career in the Salvation Army, however, was tragically short-lived. After only

The Salvation Army's first brass band – the Fry family of Salisbury,
Wiltshire.

two years he was taken ill and died in Glasgow on 24 August
1882. The band was dissolved. In this brief but glorious period
he had sown seeds that were even then beginning to show signs
of the rich musical harvest that was to follow.

In the early 1880s the number of bands was rapidly increasing.

By the middle of that decade it was estimated that there were in the region of 400 bands throughout the British Isles. There was, meanwhile, dispute over which corps could claim the distinction of having possessed the first band. Salisbury naturally laid claim and while the Fry family were there they were undoubtedly the Salisbury Corps Band, but on their departure for London the Salisbury Corps was left with only individual players and no properly organized band. Northwich in Cheshire, about whose band an article had appeared in *War Cry*, the Army's own newspaper, on 4 September, 1880 then claimed the honour. And so did Consett in Co. Durham. The conflict over these competing claims continued for several years until eventually in 1906 an official inquiry was held to consider the rival claims and finally settle the matter. The inquiry found evidence that, while the Northwich band dated back to 1880, there had been a small band in active operation with the Consett corps during the latter part of 1879. Consett, therefore, gained the honour by a short blast.

While William Booth had been cautious in his acceptance of bands, he was also strict in determining their purpose and in their discipline. Their original purpose had been to draw attention to the missioners and assist the singing both on the march and in the mission hall meetings. He issued an edict in 1884 in which he ordained that 'they are to work for the good of the corps and for the salvation of souls, and for nothing else. We are not going to stick them up on the platform nor march them through the streets for them to perform and to be admired'. The general added: 'The man must blow his cornet and shut his eyes and believe while he plays that he is blowing salvation into somebody and doing something that will be some good. Let him go on believing while he hits the drum or blows his cornet . . .'

It was a high standard to accept and maintain, yet the founder's original intention remains in force, continued today by his successors. That fact alone must speak legends about the founder's rectitude. The discipline and dedication he called for has proved too rigid for some bandsmen; the Army's loss is often a gain to secular bands. The Army's bandsmen are unpaid: indeed, they even pay a subscription to belong to a band and they buy their own uniforms. Major Norman Bearcroft, who is currently the national secretary for bands and songsters, believes that 'our strength depends upon the devotion of our bandsmen to the cause. That is what has kept us so strong all these years'.

The number of bands was increasing at a pace, but the void left by Charles Fry's death was unfilled for several years. Herbert

Booth, third son of the founder, however, formed a new musical group in 1887 bearing the strongly militarist title of the Household Troops Band. Its purpose, like that of Fry's band, was to spearhead evangelical campaigns: much of its music was performed on the march. Its musicians had to be dedicated and hardy: in one 12–month period they travelled more than 3,000 miles – and half that distance was accomplished on foot.

By now, Booth's evangelism had spread abroad. The band crossed the Atlantic in 1888 and after campaigning in Canada for five months went on to the United States for a further two months of campaigning. In 1891 the band was enlarged and for three months they played twice a day on the sands at Margate where, despite the founder's edict about not performing to be admired, they became one of the popular attractions of the resort, with the railway companies inviting Londoners to enjoy not only Margate's healthy air but to hear the band as well. The band achieved a high standard of performance through the constant practice and the simplicity of its renderings rather than displays of technical ability. Its pioneering achievement was to prove that Salvation Army band music could, according to Richard Slater, who became known as the father of Salvation Army music, 'arrest, impress and give satisfaction to the musically cultured as well as gain the attention of the average man and woman'. The band existed for six years until it was dissolved in 1893. Two years earlier the International Staff Band had been created from a nucleus of former junior bandsmen at the London headquarters whose boyhood days were over. It was to become in time the Salvation Army's premier band, known as its name implies throughout the world and ranking among the finest of brass bands.

Members of the International Staff Band all have jobs in the Army's headquarters in London or at other Army offices near enough to enable them to attend the daily half-hour rehearsals. As one of the larger Army bands it has more players than most secular bands – 36 members compared with the standard 24 in 'outside' bands. Their LP records are now to be found in record shops alongside the recordings of championship bands – again despite the strictures of the founder about not attracting admiration. Times change, even in the Salvation Army. Major Bearcroft admits to a certain ambiguity here but adds: 'Bands are intended to attract people. If a band is not entertaining, people will not come'.

Playing in an Army band, particularly in the early days, was not without its dangers. Marching and playing outdoors often offended against local bye-laws and bandsmen were frequently fined and sometimes sent to prison as a result of their activities. This type of offence was not only confined to Britain: similar punishments – and prejudices – were experienced by the pioneering missioners in America and elsewhere. The first official Salvation Army band in the United States was formed in New York in 1887. It made a spectacular first appearance on Broadway on tandem bicycles, one man pedalling while the other played, and carrying banners proclaiming themselves the 'Blowing Troubadors of God'.

The visit in 1888 of the Household Troops Band had made a great impact and created an awareness of the power of brass bands which resulted in the creation of a number of other bands in both America and Canada. The creation of similar bands was assisted in the early years of the century by the large number of immigrants arriving from Europe, many of whom were experienced bandsmen. A Canadian Staff Band was launched in 1907 which built up a good reputation, but it was disastrously extinguished seven years later. The band had embarked for England to attend an International Congress in London when, early in the morning of 29 May, 1914, their ship – the *Empress of Ireland* – and a Norwegian collier collided in fog. Within 14 minutes the *Empress of Ireland* had sunk, most of the members of the band perishing in the disaster. It was an experience from which the Canadian Salvationists never fully recovered. Their Staff Band has never been replaced.

South America, where Salvation Army work began in 1890, was slower to adopt brass bands, although small groups of instrumentalists were formed for specific occasions. The first permanent uniformed band in that continent was not set up until 1911. A brass band was first formed in Australia in 1881 in Adelaide, the first band south of the Equator. Others soon followed, including one at Melbourne in 1890 which eventually became the Australian Staff Band. Australia also had a women's band, formed in 1905, and in New Zealand, where at one time there were as many as 60 bands, there was also a Lassies' Band.

Bands were also springing up in various parts of Europe at the same time. This rapid development of evangelistic music needed to be coordinated from the London headquarters where an International Music Board was set up in 1896 to approve the music. A series of band tune books have been produced from the wealth of music specially composed for Army bands. From the material submitted to the board and tested by the International Staff Band more than 50 compositions are approved every year and added to the bands' vast repertoire. Most of the new compositions are now the work of professional composers. It was the declared ambition of Bramwell Booth, the founder's eldest son, to create the Salvation Army's own culture in music and words. This aim was assisted by a slight relaxation of the founder's original strict guidelines to permit the use of band music for which no words had been written. It had the effect of encouraging composers to write expressly for Salvation Army bands.

When the Fry family's musical campaigning abruptly ended with the death of Charles Fry, his eldest son Fred was asked to produce music to cater for the needs of the increasing number of corps bands. His had been the arrangements used by the Fry band to accompany the missionary songsters. He became a combination of composer and compositor when a second-hand printing press and two founts of mixed up musical type were bought and he was instructed to put the type in order and learn how to set it up to print Army music. A music department was set up in 1883 with a staff of three: Richard Slater, a young musician of great ability who had played first violin under Sir Arthur Sullivan in the Royal Albert Hall Amateur Orchestral Society, Fred Fry and Henry Hill, a retired police sergeant from Hull who had been bandmaster to several corps bands. Between them they produced volumes of tunes arranged for accompanying the singing. Much of it was printed lithographically from Fry's hand-written copy.

These early musicians were, however, not content merely to provide musical accompaniment for the singing, and in 1901 the founder was prevailed upon to permit the use of music without words. Slater submitted three specimen compositions. The foundation was thus laid for the now enormous repertoire of marches and sacred music. Much of this music has been composed by officers on the staff of the music department. Slater himself was a prolific composer: other staff composers of merit have included Fred Hawkes, Arthur Godsmith, Bramwell Coles, whose marches earned him the title of the Army's Souza, and, in more recent times, Eric Ball whose compositions have earned him an international reputation in both spheres, Albert Jakeway, Ray Steadman-Allen and Leslie Condon. Composers outside the department have also made a lasting impression on the Army's music: George Marshall and Herbert Twitchin in Britain, Klaus Ostby in Scandinavia, Dean Goffin (who has also written for secular bands) in New Zealand. Among the Army composers are two officers who subsequently achieved the highest office of General – William

Kitching, a well-established composer and arranger before his high appointment, and Albert Osborn.

Women have always had a role in Salvation Army bands. Here are the Case family, father, mother and two daughters, who formed the nucleus of the Portsmouth S.A. Band, formed in 1880.

Women have always had a place in the Army's music-making. It can claim at least two women composers: Captain Ruby Palon of the United States Western Territory who, in 1948, became the first woman Salvationist to have a band arrangement published, and Diane Martin of New York, who became the second in 1964. Mrs Maisie Wiggins, the first woman Bandmaster in the British territory, was the first student to become an associate of the Royal Manchester College of Music in trombone playing and played principal trombone in the Hallé Orchestra.

Many personalities in the wider musical profession have taken part in Army music festivals and have been generous in their praise of Salvation Army bands. Some have been so impressed by the Army's music and performances that they have themselves written works especially for them.

The great American march composer, John Philip Souza, had great respect for Army musicians and, at the request of General Booth, wrote a march on the occasion of the Salvation Army's golden jubilee celebrations in New York. It was called simply *The Salvation Army* and included the founder's song, *O boundless salvation*. Soon after the first performance of that work by a massive collection of 300 musicians, conducted by the composer, Souza said of Army musicians: 'If you want to know one of the very good reasons why the world needs bands, just ask one of the Salvation Army warriors who for years have marched carrying the message of the Cross through the back alleys of life. Let them tell you of the armies of men who have been turned to a better life by first hearing the sounds of a Salvation Army band. The next time you hear a Salvation Army band, no matter how humble, take off your hat.'

Men were not only turned to a better life morally by the sounds of an Army band: others were turned towards music. Dr Meredith Wilson, composer of American stage and screen musicals, who wrote *Banners and Bonnets* for the Army, began his musical career playing the drum in a Salvation Army band at Mason City, Iowa. President Theodore Roosevelt, discussing brass bands with William Booth, once told the founder: 'There is no more effective method of evangelizing people than with a brass band. I confess I like brass bands – and I like your brass bands.'

George Bernard Shaw was a strong defender and supporter of Army brass bands and frequently spoke in their defence in the days when they were less well thought of than is now the case. The first Army gathering he attended was a memorial service in the Royal Albert Hall in 1905. He came away particularly impressed by the music; he felt the Salvation Army bands had a particular affinity with the music of Handel. Of that first occasion he recalled: 'Massed Salvation Army bands played the *Dead March from Saul* as I verily believe it had never been played in the world since Handel was alive to conduct it. I have heard Handel's great march snivelled through and droned through by expensive professional bands until the thought of death became intolerable. The Salvationists, quite instinctively and probably knowing little of Handel, made it a magnificent paean of victory and glory that sent me – a seasoned music critic of many years standing – almost out of my senses with enthusiasm'.

That rendering of the *Funeral March* obviously made a lasting impression on Shaw. In a letter to Mr Kenneth Cook, the author of *The Bandsmans' Everything Within*, Shaw recalled the excellence of the playing of the International Staff Band, adding: 'Only twice in my life have I heard the *Funeral March* from Saul played as it can and should be played. Once was by the International Staff Band at a service in the Albert Hall and other was by the organist of Westminster Abbey at the funeral of Thomas Hardy.

Whoever has not heard the massed bands of the Salvation Army at their festival has missed an instructive experience'.

The following year Shaw was invited to exercise his critical skills in a private report of the bands' performances at an Army festival. Of the technique required of Salvationist musicians he commented: 'It is not enough for a Salvation Army band to play one of its scores technically well. You have only to hand the band part to Mr Souza's [band] or the Band of the Grenadier Guards and they will play it equally well. But there should be an emotional difference. It should be possible for a blindfold critic to say which was the Salvation Army band and which was the professional.' On another occasion he said: 'I consider that Salvation Army bands are among the best. Because of their fervour the Salvationists get more out of their instruments than many professional bands.'

He paid another tribute to Army bands in October 1941 when he wrote in *The Times*: 'Had the Albert Hall, the BBC Orchestra and the Salvation Army's International Staff Band been within Handel's reach the score of *Messiah* would have been of a very different specification. The music would not and could not have been better, but the instrumentation would have been much richer and more effective'.

With such high praise it is worth reflecting on what might have been the effect if Salvation Army bands had ever been permitted to take part in competitive music-making. Their strict rules ordain that they may only play music that is published by their own music department and, in turn, that music may only be sold to Army bands. The strict observance of these rules is often regretted by bandsmen who believe that much of the Army's music merits a wider audience. 'Music is music', Michel Antrobus, former resident conductor of Black Dyke Mills Band, said to me when we discussed the subject, 'and a good deal of Army music is good. Take some of Eric Ball's Army compositions – *King of Kings* for example. That is a piece of music worthy of being performed by the very best bands. Surely it is worth performing for its sheer magic by a band with the capability of Black Dyke.'

Prelude on Three Welsh Hymn Tunes, which Vaughan Williams wrote and dedicated to the Salvation Army in 1955, is another example of a piece of music which ought to have a wider performance: indeed, there is an organ version available. But the original brass band version is sacrosanct, jealously guarded by the Salvation Army, much to the regret of outside bands. Special permission can be sought to play some of these items. It has been given for the Vaughan Williams work, but this is rare. The most recent occasion of permission being granted was for a concert by the National Youth Brass Band which followed the annual course in August 1979.

How extensively the specialized musical movement of the Salvation Army has developed during its history can be seen from the number of bandsmen now involved. Throughout the world, playing in bands of varying sizes and ability, there are now more than 40,000 senior bandsmen. In Britain there are more than 720 senior bands comprising nearly 15,000 musicians, with a reserve of over 1,500 players. In addition, in England alone there are 329 junior bands with 5,357 members. The future of Salvation Army bands must, therefore, be secure. It all makes up what is arguably the most extensive and most self-contained organization of dedicated music and song producers in the world.

'Blowing troubadours of God' – the International Staff Band of the Salvation Army photographed outside their headquarters with St Paul's Cathedral in the background.

The influence of Salvation Army bands throughout the world has been profound and significant, introducing the sound of music and music-making to thousands of people. In many instances this early introduction to brass instruments and music has subsequently been of benefit to the secular bands. The Salvation Army's contribution to music is one for which the brass band movement as a whole must forever be grateful.

The top bands

The profiles which follow of some of the leading brass bands are a personal selection and the list is not intended to be comprehensive. There are other bands which some readers may think ought to have been included; perhaps some are there which other readers might prefer to have seen omitted. They are listed alphabetically and not in any particular order of merit.

Besses o' th' Barn Band

Besses is believed to have started originally as a string band before 1818, when it was known as Clegg's Band. Clegg, who provided the initial impetus to its formation, was a local employer. It broke away, however, to become a village band and was one of the first bands to indulge in contesting as early as 1821. It became an all-brass band in 1853. Between 1854 and 1892 alone, the band is reputed to have won over £1,500, an incredibly large sum in those days, from contesting. Its finances were thus already placed on a firm foundation which has been maintained.

William Rimmer started his banding career with Besses as a cornet player in the late 1880s. Rivalry between the Lancashire band and the Black Dyke Mills Band from Yorkshire mirrored the cricketing wars of the roses between the two counties. Throughout its history Besses has retained its independence. In 1885 its members purchased their own premises, which became the Besses o' th' Barn Band Social Club Union.

By 1892 it held every challenge cup then awarded to brass bands. Its successes resulted in heavy demand for concert performances. J. Henry Iles, the brass band entrepreneur, took it on a 'missionary' tour of England, Scotland and Wales in 1904, to France the following year, and on a comprehensive world tour in 1906-7. Many other tours have been undertaken in the following years.

Alexander Owen, composer of numerous popular arrangements, took over the band in 1884. These were the great days of own choice contest pieces and for the next two years the band played Owens' *Reminiscences of Rossini* on every possible occasion, including 19 contests (of which it won 14, was three times placed second, and third on two occasions). Such reliance on a particular musical item left bands open to the criticism that they were a one-tune band. On one occasion contest officials brought in a rule to prevent Besses playing the Rossini selection because it had won the contest with the same item the previous year. Owen angrily went off and produced a new selection, this time of Beethoven's works, and the band confounded its critics by gaining a joint first place.

Like most bands, Besses has had its share of ups and downs on the contest scene. Concert tours kept the band out of contests for 14 years in the early 1900s through the amateur status qualifications, but by 1918 it was back again and in 1923 set a new trend by performing at Belle Vue in concert formation instead of the long established practice of playing while standing in a square formation.

The Second World War inevitably had a lasting effect upon the band: in 1953 it performed at only one engagement in the entire year. But, reinvigorated, it began to recapture some of its former glory. During the 1960s it was among the handful of bands commissioning new works and appearing at some of the major music festivals. It is a traditional band with a modern outlook. Now, with Roy Newsome as musical director, Besses is a formidable force again in contesting and a popular concert band.

Black Dyke Mills Band

While it may not be quite the oldest, Black Dyke Mills Band is probably the best and certainly the most consistently successful band still in existence. With Besses, it is one of the bands that have survived from the great pioneering days in the second decade of the last century. In its early days it was a mixture of reed and brass instruments. John Foster, founder of the Mills, while not the originator of the band, was a horn player with it when it was known as Peter Wharton's Band. The original band suffered the inevitable loss of members but re-emerged in 1833, again as a reed and brass band. It was among the 12 bands which competed in the finals of the first championships at Crystal Palace in 1860, taking one of the prizes on the first day and thus being excluded from performing on the second day of the meeting.

In 1879 the legendary conductor and trainer, Alexander Owen, first became associated with the band. Since the 1850s the band has enjoyed generous support from the proprietors of the mill. Nowadays, only three members of the band actually work in the mill. One, an organ builder, worked on the rebuilding of the York Minster organ, another is managing director of a local building firm, and several are teachers. The band's president, Mr Peter Lambert, is a director of the mill.

To brass band enthusiasts, Black Dyke Band has a sound of its own. Michael Antrobus, a former resident conductor, told the author he had never heard a sound like it, even in the orchestral brass field, and recalled how, when he conducted them in the *Downland Suite* during a visit to Norway in 1979, he 'just stood on the rostrum, closed my eyes and let it all happen: it was a tremendous experience'. It is said the inimitable sound has something to do with the acoustics of their bandroom, which has been in use since the band's inception. In 1979, however, the firm spent £40,000 on rebuilding and refurbishing the room, but any super-stitions about the effects of the changes on the 'sound of Dyke' were dispelled when the band that year carried off both the British national and European championship awards.

Black Dyke is a band with high standards and strict discipline. No excuses, other than a doctor's note in the case of genuine illness, are accepted for failure to attend the twice weekly rehearsals. High standards and consistency are demanded from the players and their conductor. Their repertoire for a concert season is planned 12 months ahead. In the contesting sphere, the band's record is unapproachable by any other band: since 1860 it has won the British Open championship on 22 occasions, been placed second on 12 occasions and third on 10. In the national championships, it has been in first place on 14 appearances since 1900, world champions in 1970 and European champions in 1978 and 1979, in which latter year it was also national champion band.

With such a long history most of the famous names of the brass band world have been associated with the band at some period. Some have become legendary figures, like Arthur O. Pearce who was appointed bandmaster in 1912 and was conductor for many years until his retire-ment in 1948. During that period the band won over £12,500 in prizes. Another of its characters was John Paley, who played principal cornet for many years and was nationally known as a soloist, having initially achieved eminence when he played a solo at the first Crystal Palace festival in 1900. Paley was a publican in a suburb of nearby Bradford and there are people still alive who recall how he would throw up a window and give an impromptu performance to his fans in the street below.

Brighouse and Rastrick Band

Five miles down the road from the Queensbury headquarters of Black Dyke Mills Band is the home of their local rivals, the Brighouse and Rastrick Band. Unlike Black Dyke, with its long history of patronage, Brighouse and Rastrick has always been a subscription band – probably the most successful subscription band in the history of banding. Sub-scribers pay a modest annual sum, with the rest of the income coming mainly from contest prize money, the proceeds of concert arrangements, and the activities of the band committee and helpers. Twelve years ago, they bought a former parish hall in the town, Rydings Hall, as their headquarters. It has its own bars and a 500-seat concert hall. Its financial future has been secured by its unexpected and sensational rise to the top of the popular music charts in 1977 – over £50,000 was received in royalties in the first year – with the band's recording of *The Floral Dance*. This Cornish air was arranged by the band's musical director, Derek Broadbent, and, with its strong percussion beat, displayed the two main influences of his own musical experience: the rich sound of the brass band combined with the effects of the dance band. The band, as a result, has done more than any other to popularize brass bands in recent times and their example has been followed, albeit with less financial success, by many other brass bands.

There have been references to a Brighouse Band as far back as 1857 taking part in a contest in the Piece Hall Yard in nearby Halifax, which Black Dyke won and which may have inspired the long rivalry that has existed between the two bands. The existing band dates from 1860 when it was named Brighouse and Rastrick Temperance Band and consisted of brass and reed instruments. The change to all-brass came in 1881 and the temperance tag in their title was deleted in 1928.

In 1924 the band engaged as their conductor Fred Berry, who had played euphonium with a number of noted local bands and had been with Besses o' th' Barn Band on their world tour in 1906. He put the band on the national map in 1929 when they qualified for the championship section at Belle Vue for the first time and went on to win, a performance that had not previously been equalled since 1890.

Throughout the 1930s it was the most successful band in the Belle Vue contests. The band's development in the top grade came during Berry's 20 year association. After the Belle Vue victory of 1936 it had to wait 42 years before its name again appeared on the Belle Vue roll of champions in 1978, although in 1969 the band had become world champions. The 1978 success was an interesting one for at least two reasons. It deprived their old rivals, Black Dyke, of a second hat-trick. Black Dyke had also won the world championship eight years earlier playing the same test-piece, *Benvenuto Cellini* by Berlioz, under the guidance of Geoffrey Brand. Brighouse recruited Brand as their professional conductor – and won. Their victory also came at a time of controversy in the movement over their outstanding popular success with *Floral Dance* and thus demonstrated the musical adaptability and skill of the Brighouse players.

Brighouse have a distinctive sartorial appearance with their purple coloured uniforms. The Brighouse men tell a story of their Black Dyke rivals rehearsing Gilbert Vinter's *Spectrum* in which the music portrays images of various colours including purple. When the conductor urged them to 'imagine purple and feel purple' and inquired what picture the colour conjured up for them, one bandsman tartly replied 'Bloody Briggus and Rastrick'. Rivalry there may be, but bandsmen in both bands have a healthy respect for each other's musical abilities.

Just as few members of Black Dyke Band now work in the mill, the Brighouse band has only a handful of local players in its ranks. Players are happy to travel miles for the regular rehearsals and the privilege of being one of its members.

Carlton Main Frickley Colliery Band

One of the best known colliery bands in the country, Carlton Main Frickley Band comes from an area of Yorkshire as famous for its brass bands as for its coal. It is centred on South Elmsall and within a few miles are the famous Grimethorpe Colliery and Markham Main Colliery Bands. There has been a band at South Elmsall since 1898 when it started as a village band, although most of the players were miners from the nearby South Kirkby Colliery. It was adopted as a colliery band in 1905 when Frickley Colliery began to be mined. The Carlton Main Coal Company, which owned Frickley in the days of private enterprise collieries, was one of the more prosperous companies and built up the band until it had such a reputation that musical miners would leave other pits where the band was less good for the opportunity to join the Frickley band. Its first major success was to win the British Open championship in 1922, but it had to wait until 1958 to repeat its success. In the national championship it came second in 1959 and again in 1960, but the crown has since eluded them. In the annual Mineworkers' contest it has had a highly successful double decade with three wins in the 1960s and coming second or third almost every year until it regained the title in 1978. It also won the Granada contest in 1978. Its most famous conductor for many years was Jack Atherton, who trained some of the country's best bandsmen and gave much encouragement to young players in particular.

C.W.S. (Manchester) Band

The Cooperative Movement has long been among brass band patrons and one of the most successful bands to emerge is the C.W.S. (Manchester) Band.

On its formation in 1901 it was known as the C.W.S. Tobacco Factory Band and became known by its present title in 1938. After the war, directors of the Cooperative Wholesale Society took over responsibility for the band from the workers' committee which had previously run it. The band was revitalized with players from other bands and Eric Ball, who had then ended his full-time association with the Salvation Army, was appointed professional conductor. In a short time the band was scaling the championship heights. Its first taste of national glory came in 1948 when, with Eric Ball conducting, the band won the British Open championship at Belle Vue. They were back in first place again four years later. In 1954 the late Alex Mortimer, one of the members of the famous banding family, began a lengthy association with the band, which was unfortunately brought to a close through the ill-health of the conductor who, latterly, had conducted from a wheel chair. Under his baton, the band achieved a series of important successes in contests and a very good reputation for concert work during the 1950s and 1960s. It came second to Brighouse in the National Championships of 1973.

Cory Band

Cory Band, from the Rhondda Valley in South Wales, is one of the oldest and the premier Welsh band. It was founded in 1887 in Ton Petre and later became the Ton Temperance Band. In 1895, however, it was taken over by Mr (later Sir) Clifford J. Cory, who was so impressed by their performance that he offered the band financial help if they became the works band of the Cory Brothers Coal Company. The name was then changed to Cory Workmens' Band. It was one of the first brass bands to broadcast in July 1923 with a performance from a studio in Cardiff.

Under Professor Walter Hargreaves, the band had a successful period after the Second World War when he took them to second place in the national championship in 1948 and to a similar place in the British Open two years later, but it was from the early 1970s that it really emerged as a potent force. It became the first band to take the national championship title over the border to Wales in 1974, and it has battled with Grimethorpe Colliery Band through the early years of the decade for the main title in the Mineworkers' championships. These rivalries were set aside, however, in 1976 when the two bands became musical ambassadors for a tour of America as part of the bi-centennial celebrations.

Most of their success was under the conductorship of Major H. A. Kenney. By the mid-1970s their players with connections with the coal-mining industry had dwindled to such an extent that they were no longer eligible under the 50 per cent membership rule to compete in the Mineworkers' contest where so many of their successes had been achieved. They have latterly been meeting with further success in other contests under the guidance of Denzil Stephens.

Desford Colliery Band

Desford Colliery Band hails from the Midlands coalfield. Formed at the end of the last century as Ibstock United Band it has had several different tiles but it has gained most of its support from miners. Over 60 per cent of the players are engaged in mining, the shift working of which creates difficulties for rehearsals and engagements.

The band is now sponsored by the Dowty Mining Company at Tewkesbury, Gloucestershire. It has undertaken concert tours in Europe, particularly Germany, which it visited in 1977 and 1978. In that latter year one of its young members, principal solo cornet player Kevin Dye, won the solo championship of Great Britain.

The band has maintained a consistently good standard of performance which earned it a well-justified place as runner-up in the 1979 British Open championship, only one point behind the winners, Fairey Engineering Works Band. It is also one of the main contenders in the annual Mineworkers' championships.

Fairey Engineering Works Band

Fairey Engineering Works Band has been a force to be reckoned with since its formation in 1937 by Sir Richard Fairey and the manager of his Stockport (Cheshire) works, Major Barlow. It was known until recently as Fairey Aviation Works Band.

On its formation, Harry Mortimer, who was then still playing the cornet under his father's baton with Fodens Motor Works Band, was invited to be musical director: thus began a 40–year association with the band which lasted until 1978. Within a year of its formation, the band was playing in the championship section and won their first major contest in 1941. At the outset all the players were employed in the factory but, as with most other works bands, this is no longer the case.

The band has been prominently placed in the major contests over the past 30 years or more and has produced during that time many distinguished players who have moved on to become musical directors of · other famous bands.

It is a band with a reputation for establishing records of long service. In addition to Harry Mortimer's long association, only four men have played solo euphonium since the band was formed and at one period the same trombone section remained intact for 17 years. Not many bands can show service of that order. In 1978 Professor Walter Hargreaves, a veteran band trainer and conductor, was appointed musical director and took them to victory again as British Open champions on their home ground of Belle Vue in 1979. It was, surprisingly, the veteran conductor's first Open championship win and he cajoled from the band what the judges regarded as a 'beautifully controlled performance – fine music-making – technically assured, brilliantly executed and directed throughout with verve and musicianship'. Fine tributes to conductor and players alike and proof that Fairey is still a force in the contest field.

Fodens Motor Works Band

Edwin Foden's ambition was to have the best brass band in the world. He had been one of the founders of the Elworth village band near his motor-wagon works at Sandbach, Cheshire, but this foundered in 1902 and Foden took over the remnants, recruited some fine players, got rid of those who were not good enough and set about achieving his ambition. He had also recruited the finest band trainer of the time, William Rimmer. The band reached the championship class at their first attempt and won the British Open championship in 1909. William Halliwell then took over and in 1910 led them to a notable double victory – the British Open and the national championships. Less successful bands were envious of their successes and the band was criticized over its recruitment of players. But Fodens claimed that all the bandsmen were employed in the works: their only advantage over other bands was their ability to pay for the best training, and the enthusiasm of the bandsmen.

Edwin Foden did not live to achieve his ambition. He died in 1911 before the band he had created achieved its greatest days. But his sons, who succeeded him, were equally enthusiastic.

A reconstruction of the band took place in 1918 following the effects of the First World War. The band survived management changes and 1929 saw the beginning of an era in which they made a tremendous impact on the band scene. In that year Fred Mortimer became musical director, being joined by his three talented sons, Alex, Harry and Rex. It was a formidable family combination. The years ahead were those in which, it was said, bets were placed not on which band would win the championships but which would come second to Fodens. Fred Mortimer imposed a strict disciplinary regime (his son, Harry Mortimer, has described him as 'a martinet'); because of unemployment resulting from the economic conditions of the period, bandsmen had little choice but to accept his rule which, it had to be admitted, paid dividends in the band's musical successes. It achieved three championship hat-tricks in a 12–year period. A new rule which barred bands with three successive wins from participating in the next championship kept them out of the planned 1939 contest. The war intervened, however, and that year's national championships were cancelled but, much to the disgust of the band, the ban was extended to apply in the first post-war championship in 1945.

The Mortimer family's connection with the band continued after Fred Mortimer's death in 1953: Harry Mortimer conducted the band until 1956 when he was appointed musical adviser (a post he held until 1979), and his brother Rex became musical director.

Championship successes have been less numerous in recent years, but the band has maintained its reputation. In 1975 it reached a watershed when financial stringency in the firm caused a careful examination of the band's position and future. The company decided to continue its support, although the musical director's post was made a part-time appointment. It remains one of the leading bands nevertheless.

Grimethorpe Colliery Band

A small hall behind the Grimethorpe and Ferrymoor Miners' Welfare Club is the headquarters of the Grimethorpe Colliery Band. Over the door is a sign proudly proclaiming it to be the home of 'The Famous Grimethorpe Colliery Band'. Within the unprepossessing surroundings of that hall, Grimethorpe has in the 1970s carried out musical experiments which have almost revolutionized the brass band movement.

Formed during the First World War after the demise of the Cudworth Band from the next village and with help from the colliery institute committee and a fund started by the colliery company, the bandsmen all work in the colliery. It is supported financially by the miners themselves, each miner paying a contribution to the colliery welfare fund of which a quarter goes to the band. Its prize money and concert engagement fees also swell the funds. It is also fortunate in having the wholehearted support of the colliery manager and area Coal Board officials who allow time for rehearsals and engagements. Some other colliery bands less fortunate view such support enviously.

The band has a creditable record in contests, but since 1972 when Elgar Howarth became its professional musical director it has built up a distinguished reputation for its concert performances. Under his influence the band has commissioned works – often controversial – from new composers and has not hesitated to indulge in musical experimentation. The experience of being propelled from the cosy atmosphere of the traditional brass band repertoire into a new world of *avant-garde* music has been taken by the bandsmen in their stride. The new music is frequently more demanding technically and when a particular piece of music requires a break with the conventional, the band has made changes in formation. This has all created controversy among the traditionalists but at the same time has done a service to the brass band movement by both extending the repertoire way beyond the traditional fare into previously unthought of realms of musical performance and the reputation of brass bands beyond the barriers which had long inhibited the movement.

In 1974 Grimethorpe shared with Black Dyke Mills Band the privilege of being the first brass bands to take part in the Proms in the Royal Albert Hall, where the noisy enthusiasm of the promenaders contrasted with the quiet concentration of the audience at the brass band championships in the same hall. The band has followed this up with numerous appearances at major music festivals and other musical events. It has exerted an influence on the brass band movement which will long be felt.

G.U.S. Band

The G.U.S. Band has had several guises in its life. It started in 1933 as Munn and Felton's Works Band from the centre of the footwear industry in Kettering, Northamptonshire. Two of the directors, the brothers F.S. and A.S. Felton, were brass band enthusiasts who were determined to have a good quality band. Stanley Boddington, now retired from active banding but still a respected conductor, was then working for the firm and was approached by the Felton brothers and told of their intentions. There were, they said, about 16 brass players employed by the firm. Mr Boddington, who had been brought up in Salvation Army bands in the area, was invited to be conductor; it was only in 1975 that he retired as musical director. William Halliwell became the professional trainer and conductor and within two years of its formation he had the G.U.S. firmly established among the leading bands. Only a year after being formed it had won first place in the second section and the following year, with Fodens unable to compete because of its three successive wins, the Kettering band emerged as national champions, overtaking bands like Black Dyke Mills, which was placed third and Besses o' th' Barn which was fourth. The local newspaper proudly proclaimed their success as 'one of the biggest sensations in brass band history ... Nothing as remarkable as the Kettering band's success has ever occurred ... '

The Second World War left the band denuded with only four players. It was revived after the war and quickly re-established itself as a leading band. Changes in management in the early 1960s when the firm became part of the Great Universal Stores group brought a change of title to the cumbrous G.U.S. (Footwear) Band and an outstanding reputation in both contest and concert work. They were named twice on the championship trophy during the 1960s and were world champions in 1971. Gilbert Vinter, the composer, was a great admirer of the band and he composed several items for its highly successful G.U.S. Quartet. Further changes in management and administration in the later 1970s brought another change of name: 'footwear' was dropped from the title and it became the G.U.S. Band. Early in 1980 there came another change of name to Great Universal Band. Despite the changes it has been able to maintain high standards, but has been less successful in contests than in the post-war era.

Hammonds Sauce Works Band

Hammonds Sauce Works Band from Shipley, West Yorkshire, is one of the most successful of post-war bands. It was started in 1946 by the managing director, H.B. Hawley, who had for many years been a leading figure in the brass band scene in Yorkshire. He had at one time been a player in the village band at Grassington, in the Yorkshire Dales, and in

1926 had been one of the founders of the Harrogate and District Brass Band Association. Mr Hawley, who was largely a self-taught musician, had also played with the nearby Saltaire Band. When that famous old band dissolved, he took over the instruments and library, had a rehearsal room built at his works and set about creating a new band which was initially composed of 18 teenage boys. After only a year they began contesting and within a decade had progressed through the various grades to become finalists in the national championship. Mr Hawley's musical talents extended to composing rousing march tunes, several of which are still important items in the band's repertoire. It is still a youthful band in its composition and the firm also supports two junior bands. The 'B' band, as it was previously known, was in 1979 re-named as the Hawley Band in honour of the Hawley family and its support of brass bands.

The band is a popular concert band and has made many broadcasts, television appearances and recordings. Since 1966 Geoffrey Whitham, who was euphonium soloist for many years with Black Dyke Mills Band, has been the band's musical director and under his leadership the band has become established among the best in Yorkshire brass bands.

Sun Life Stanshawe Band

Stanshawe Band is one of the great success stories of the 1970s. A group of musicians in Bristol was dissatisfied with brass band music standards in the area and in 1968 formed the Stanshawe Band. They started with second-hand instruments bought with the help of local businessmen. Walter Hargreaves, the veteran conductor and trainer, then accepted an invitation to become professional conductor. He moulded the band into the style in which it has developed and he merits much of the praise for its subsequent successes. Under his guidance the band won the Granada contest in 1974 and came second in the British Open championship in the same year. They came second in the national championship the following year, were BBC Band of the Year in 1977 and won the BBC Best of Brass contest in 1979. The band obtained sponsorship from the Sun Life Assurance Society Ltd in 1978, whose name was then incorporated in the band's title. Derek Bourgeois, the composer, who is a lecturer in music at Bristol University, became the band's professional conductor in 1980.

Wingates Temperance Band

Wingates Temperance Band is another of the famous bands which dates back to the pioneering days of banding and has survived. It came into existence in 1873 when members of a Bible class at Wingates Independent Methodist Chapel suspended their customary religious meeting to discuss a challenge by members of Westhoughton Old Band. Like most bands it has had its lean years but has come through financial and other crises and, for more than 70 years, has been one of the foremost bands in the movement.

It has throughout been an independent band, relying for its finances on prize money, concert fees and the efforts of members and supporters, of whom there are many. (It now has around 100 beneficent vice-presidents.)

At the start it was an offspring of the temperance movement: some of its founders were said to have been shocked at the sight of bandsmen at the head of a procession creeping into a local hostelry to sustain themselves and to have decided then to form their own band. The temperance label was retained more in the cause of tradition than outright belief in teetotalism, but it was finally dropped from the name in 1980.

Towards the end of the last century an adjudicator described Wingates as 'a good band with poor instruments'. As their instruments had cost the band the then large sum of £150, the bandsmen did not take kindly to such a back-handed compliment. It is an illustration of the rising cost of instruments that the band had to spend £6,000 on re-equipping with new instruments to mark its centenary in 1973.

The band had its struggles in the early days but when they eventually struck gold they did it in a suitably dramatic way. After being placed third in the first national championship in 1900 and being among the leaders in succeeding years, the top prize eluded them for six years – but in 1906 and 1907 they won both the national and British Open championships. Three years later the band was almost devastated when eight of its players were among the 344 men and boys killed in a local colliery disaster.

Wingates has been constantly in the prize lists apart from a spell in the 1950s, but they have fought back and during the 1970s it was the only band to break the Yorkshire stranglehold on the British Open championships.

Yorkshire Imperial Band

The Yorkshire 'Imps' Band, as it is affectionately known, was formed in 1936 when it was known as the Yorkshire Copper Works Band. An industrial merger in 1958 brought a new title, the Band of Yorkshire Imperial Metals, but this was changed again in 1980 to Yorkshire Imperial Band.

After a lean period in terms of awards the band has appeared among the leading bands in the country since the 1950s and is now one of the foremost bands in Britain.

It has had successive wins at Belle Vue in the years 1970 and 1971 but, despite high placings, it was not until 1978 that it managed to take the national title back to Leeds. Its record shows it, however, to be one of the most consistent of bands.

Championship winners

British Open Champions

1853 **Mossley Temperance** (W. Taylor)
(Two own choice selections)

1854 Leeds Railway Foundry (Richard Smith)
(Two own choice selections)

1855 Accrington (Radcliffe Barnes)
(*Orynthia*, Melling and one own
choice selection)

1856 Leeds Railway Foundry (Richard Smith)
(*Stradella* Overture, Flotow, and one
own choice selection)

1857 Leeds (Smith's) (Richard Smith) (*Il Trovatore*, Verdi, and one own
choice selection)

1858 Accrington (Radcliffe Barnes)
(Items from *Creation*, Haydn)

1859 No contest: cancelled because only three bands entered

1860 Halifax 4th West Yorkshire Rifle
Volunteers
(*Zampa*, Hérold, and one own choice selection)

1861 Halifax 4th West Yorkshire Rifle Volunteers
(*Satanella*, Balfe, and one own choice selection)

1862 Black Dyke Mills (Samuel Longbottom)
(*Muette de Portici*, Auber, and one own choice
selection)

1863 Black Dyke Mills (Samuel Longbottom)
(*Faust*, Gounod, and one own choice selection)

1864 Bacup (John Lord)
(*Reminiscences of Auber* and one own choice
selection)

1865 Bacup (John Lord)
(*Un Ballo in Maschera*, Verdi, and one own choice
selection)

1866 Dewsbury (John Peel)
(*L'Africaine*, Meyerbeer, and one own choice selection)

1867 Clay Cross (John Naylor)
(*Der Freischutz*, Weber)

1868 Burnley 17th Lancs Rifle Volunteers
(*Robert le Diable*, Meyerbeer)

1869 Bacup (John Lord)
(*Le Prophete*, Meyerbeer)

1870 Bacup (John Lord)
(*Ernani*, Verdi)

1871 Black Dyke Mills (Samuel Longbottom)
(*Il Barbiere*, Rossini)

1872 Robin Hood Rifles (H. Leverton)
(*Souvenir de Mozart*)

1873 Meltham Mills (John Gladney)
(*Dinorah*, Meyerbeer)

1874 Linthwaite (Edwin Swift)
(*Faust*, Spohr)

1875 Kingston Mills (John Gladney)
(*Il Talismano*, Balfe)

1876 Meltham Mills (John Gladney)
(*Aida*, Verdi)

1877 Meltham Mills (John Gladney)
(*Jessonda*, Spohr)

1878 Meltham Mills (John Gladney)
(*Romeo et Giulietta*, Gounod)

1879 Black Dyke Mills (J. Fawcett)
(*The Last Judgment*, Spohr)

1880 Black Dyke Mills (Alexander Owen)
(*Vespri Siciliana*, Verdi)

1881 Black Dyke Mills (Alexander Owen)
(*Cinq Mars*, Gounod)

1882 Clayton-le-Moor (Alexander Owen)
(*Il Seraglio*, Mozart)

1883 Littleborough Public (Edwin Swift)
(*Il Giuramento*, Mercadante)

1884 Honley (John Gladney)
(*La Gazza Ladra*, Rossini)

1885 Kingston Mills (John Gladney)
(*Nabucodonosor*, Verdi)

1886 Kingston Mills (John Gladney)
(*La Favorita*, Donizetti)

1887 Kingston Mills (John Gladney)
(*L'Etoile du Nord*, Meyerbeer)

1888 Wyke Temperance (Edwin Swift)
(*Der Fliegende Hollander*, Wagner)

1889 Wyke Temperance (Edwin Swift)
(*Le Reine de Saba*, Gounod)

1890 Batley Old (John Gladney)
(*Euryanthe*, Weber)

1891 Black Dyke Mills (John Gladney)
(*Das Nachtlager in Granada*, Kreutzer)

1892 Besses o' th' Barn (Alexander Owen)
(*Zaar and Zimmermann*, Lortzing)

1893 Kingston Mills (John Gladney)
(*Elaine*, Bemberg)

1894 Besses o' th' Barn (Alexander Owen)
(*The Golden Web*, Goring Thomas)

1895 Black Dyke Mills (John Gladney)
(*Hansel and Gretel*, Humperdinck)

1896 Black Dyke Mills (John Gladney)
(*Gabriella*, Pizzi)

1897 Mossley (Alexander Owen)
(*Moses in Egypt*, Rossini)

1898 Wyke Temperance (Edwin Swift)
(Grand Fantasia from works of Mendelssohn)

1899 Black Dyke Mills (John Gladney)
(*Aroldo*, Verdi)

1900 Lindley (John Gladney)
(*La Gioconda*, Ponchielli)

1901 Kingston Mills (John Gladney)
(*Mirella*, Gounod)

1902 Black Dyke Mills (John Gladney)
(*L'Ebreo,* Appoloni)

1903 Pemberton Old (John Gladney)
(*Carractacus*, Elgar)

1904 Black Dyke Mills (John Gladney)
(*Semiramide*, Rossini)

1905 Irwell Springs (William Rimmer)
(*Cosi Fan Tutte*, Mozart)

1906 Wingates Temperance (William Rimmer)
      (*Les Huguenots*, Meyerbeer)

1907 Wingates Temperance (William Rimmer)
      (*Robin Hood*, MacFarren)

1908 Black Dyke Mills (William Rimmer)
      (A Souvenir of Grieg)

1909 Fodens Motor Works (William Rimmer)
      (*Il Bravo*, Marliani)

1910 Fodens Motor Works (William Halliwell)
      (*Acis and Galatea*, Handel)

1911 Hebden Bridge (William Halliwell)
      (*Eugene Onegin*, Tchaikovsky)

1912 Fodens Motor Works (William Halliwell)
      (*Les Diamanta de la Couronne*, Auber)

1913 Fodens Motor Works (WIlliam Halliwell)
      (A Souvenir of Gounod)

1914 Black Dyke Mills (J.A. Greenwood)
      (*Joseph und seine Bruder*, Mehul)

1915 Fodens Motor Works (William Halliwell)
      (*Il Furioso*, Donizetti)

1916 Horwich Railway Mechanics Institute (J.A. Greenwood)
      (*La Traviata*, Verdi)

1917 Horwich R.M.I. (J.A. Greenwood)
      (*Le Pré aux Clercs*, Herold)

1918 Wingates Temperance (William Halliwell)
      (*Il Bravo*, Marliani)

1919 Harton Colliery (G. Hawkins)
      (*The Lily of Killarney*, Benedict)

1920 Besses o' th' Barn (William Wood)
      (*I Lombardi*, Verdi)

1921 Wingates Temperance (William Halliwell)
      (*Maritana*, Vincent Wallace)

1922 South Elmsall and Frickley Colliery (Noel Thorpe)
      (*Lohengrin*, Wagner)

1923 Wingates Temperance (William Halliwell)
      (*Dinorah*, Meyerbeer)

1924 Newcastle Steel Works, Australia (A.H. Bailie)
      (Selection from Franz Liszt)

1925 Creswell Colliery (J.A. Greenwood)
      (*Macbeth*, Keighley)

1926 Fodens Motor Works (William Halliwell)
      (*A Midsummer Night's Dream*, Keighley)

1927 Fodens Motor Works (William Halliwell)
      (*Merry Wives of Windsor*, Keighley)

1928 Fodens Motor Works (William Halliwell)
      (*Lorenzo*, Keighley)

1929 Brighouse and Rastrick (Fred Berry)
      (*Pathětique*, Beethoven)

1930 Eccles Borough (J. Dow)
      (*Oriental Rhapsody*, Bantock)

1931 Besses o' th' Barn (William Halliwell)
      (*Springtime*, Haydn Morris)

1932 Brighouse and Rastrick (William Halliwell)
      (*The Crusaders*, Keighley)

1933 Brighouse and Rastrick (William Halliwell)
      (*Princess Nada*, Denis Wright)

1934 Brighouse and Rastrick (William Halliwell)
      (*Pageantry*, Howells)

1935 Black Dyke Mills (William Halliwell)
      (*A Northern Rhapsody*, Keighley)

1936 Brighouse and Rastrick (William Halliwell)
(*Robin Hood*, Geehl)

1937 Besses o' th' Barn (William Wood)
(*Academic Festival Overture*, Brahms)

1938 Slaithwaite (Noel Thorpe)
(*Owain Glyndwr*, Maldwyn Price)

1939 Wingates Temperance (William Wood)
(*A Downland Suite*, Ireland)

1940 Bickershaw Colliery (William Haydock)
(*Clive of India*, Holbrooke)

1941 Fairey Aviation Works (Harry Mortimer)
(Choice of three works)

1942 Fairey Aviation Works (Harry Mortimer)
(Choice of two works)

1943 Bickershaw Colliery (William Haydock)
(Theme from Symphony No 5, Beethoven, arr.
Denis Wright)

1944 Fairey Aviation (Harry Mortimer)
(*Fantasia: The Tempest*, Johnson)

1945 Fairey Aviation (Harry Mortimer)
(*Pride of Race*, K. A. Wright)

1946 Bickershaw Colliery (Harry Mortimer)
(*Salute to Freedom*, Ball)

1947 Fairey Aviation (Harry Mortimer)
(*Tone Poem: Henry V*, Maldwyn Price)

1948 C.W.S. Manchester (Eric Ball)
(*Music for Brass*, Denis Wright)

1949 Fairey Aviation (Harry Mortimer)
(*Rhapsody in Brass*, Dean Goffin)

1950 Fairey Aviation (Harry Mortimer)
(*Resurgam*, Ball)

1951 Ransome and Marles' Works Band (Eric Ball)
(*The Conquerors*, Ball)

1952 C.W.S. Manchester (Eric Ball)
(*Scena Sinfonica*, Geehl)

1953 National Band of New Zealand (K.G.L. Smith)
(*The Three Musketeers*, Hespe)

1954 Munn and Felton (Stanley Boddington)
(*Tournament for Brass*, Ball)

1955 Ferodo Works (George Hespe)
(*Sinfonietta for Brass Band*, Leidzen)

1956 Fairey Aviation (Harry Mortimer)
(*Tam o'Shanter's Ride*, Denis Wright)

1957 Black Dyke Mills (Major G.H. Willcocks)
(*Carnival*, Helen Perkin)

1958 Carlton Main Frickley Colliery (Jack Atherton)
(*Sunset Rhapsody*, Ball)

1959 Besses o' th' Barn (William Wood)
(*The Undaunted*, Ball)

1960 C.W.S. Manchester (Alex Mortimer)
(*Fantasia*, Mozart, arr. Sargent)

1961 The Fairey Band (Leonard Lamb)
(*Main Street*, Ball)

1962 The Fairey Band (Leonard Lamb)
(*Island Heritage*, Helen Perkin)

1963 The Fairey Band (Leonard Lamb)
(*Life Divine*, Cyril Jenkins)

1964 Fodens Motor Works (Rex Mortimer)
(*Lorenzo*, Keighley)

1965 The Fairey Band (Leonard Lamb)
(*Saga of the North*, Cyril Jenkins)

1966 C.W.S. Manchester (Alex Mortimer)
(*A Downland Suite*, Ireland)

1967 Grimethorpe Colliery (George Thompson)
(*A Comedy Overture*, Ireland)

1968 Black Dyke Mills (Geoffrey Brand)
(*John O'Gaunt*, Vinter)

1969 Grimethorpe Colliery (George Thompson)
(*Spectrum*, Vinter)

1970 Yorkshire Imperial Metals (Trevor Walmsley)
(*Pageantry*, Howells)

1971 Yorkshire Imperial Metals (Trevor Walmsley)
(*Festival Music*, Ball)

1972 Black Dyke Mills (Geoffrey Brand)
(*Sovereign Heritage*, Beever)

1973 Black Dyke Mills (Roy Newsome)
(*The Accursed Huntsman*, César Franck)

1974 Black Dyke Mills (Roy Newsome)
(*James Cook – Circumnavigator*, Vinter)

1975 Wingates Temperance (Richard Evans)
(*Fireworks*, Elgar Howarth)

1976 Black Dyke Mills (Major Peter Parkes)
(*An Epic Symphony*, Percy Fletcher)

1977 Black Dyke Mills (Major Peter Parkes)
(*Diadem of Gold*, Bailey, arr. Frank Wright)

1978 Brighouse and Rastrick (Geoffrey Brand)
(*Benvenuto Cellini*, Berlioz)

1979 Fairey Engineering Works (Walter Hargreaves)
(*Le Carnaval Romain*, Berlioz)

National Champions 1900–1938

1900 **Denton Original** (Alexander Owen)
('*Gems from Sullivan's Operas No. 1*,'
arr. J. Ord Hume)

1901 **Lee Mount** (W. Swingler)
('*Gems from Sullivan's Operas No. 3*,'
arr. J. Ord Hume)

1902 **Black Dyke Mills** (J. Gladney)
('*Hiawatha*,' Coleridge-Taylor,
arr. Lt. Chas. Godfrey)

1903 **Besses o' th' Barn** (Alexander Owen)
('*Die Meistersinger*,' Wagner,
arr. Shipley Douglas)

1904 **Hebburn Colliery** (Angus Holden)
('*Gems of Mendelssohn*,'
arr. Lt. Chas. Godfrey)

1905 **Irwell Springs** (William Rimmer)
('*Roland à Roncevaux*,'
Auguste Mermet)

1906 **Wingates Temperance** (William Rimmer)
('*Gems of Chopin*,'
arr. Wm. Short)

1907 **Wingates Temperance** (William Rimmer)
('*Gems of Schumann*,'
arr. Wm. Short)

1903 **Irwell Springs** (William Rimmer)
('*Rienzi*,' arr. S. Cope)

1909 **Shaw** (William Rimmer)
('*Flying Dutchman*,' Wagner)

1910 **Fodens Motor Works** (William Halliwell)
('*Gems of Schubert*,'
arr. W. Rimmer)

1911 **Crossfield's Soap Works** (William Halliwell)
('*Les Huguenots*,' Meyerbeer,
arr. W. Rimmer)

1912 **St Hilda Colliery** (William Halliwell)
('*William Tell*,' Rossini)

1913 **Irwell Springs** (William Halliwell)
('*Labour and Love*,' Percy Fletcher)

1914–1919 None

1920 **St Hilda Colliery** (William Halliwell)
('*Coriolanus*,' Cyril Jenkins)

1921 **St Hilda Colliery** (William Halliwell)
('*Life Divine*,' Cyril Jenkins)

1922 **Horwich R. M. I.** (John Greenwood)
('*Freedom*,' Hubert Bath)

1923 **Luton Red Cross** (William Halliwell)
('*Oliver Cromwell*,' Henry Geehl)

1924 **St Hilda Colliery** (William Halliwell)
('*On the Cornish Coast*,' Henry Geehl)

1925 **Marsden Colliery** (John Greenwood)
('*Joan of Arc*,' Denis Wright)

1926 **St Hilda Colliery** (James Oliver)
('*An Epic Symphony*,' Percy Fletcher)

1927 **Carlisle St. Stephens** (William Lowes)
('*The White Rider*,' Denis Wright)

1928 **Black Dyke Mills** (William Halliwell)
('*A Moorside Suite*,' Gustav Holst)

1929 **Carlisle St. Stephens** (William Lowes)
('*Victory*,' Cyril Jenkins)

1930 **Fodens Motor Works** (Fred Mortimer)
('*Severn Suite Op. 87*,' Edward Elgar)

1931 **Wingates Temperance** (Harold Moss)
('*Honour and Glory*,' Hubert Bath)

1932 **Fodens Motor Works** (Fred Mortimer)
('*A Downland Suite*,' John Ireland)

1933 **Fodens Motor Works** (Fred Mortimer)
('*Prometheus Unbound*,' Granville Bantock)

1934 **Fodens Motor Works** (Fred Mortimer)
('*Comedy Overture*,' John Ireland)

1935 **Munn & Felton's Works** (William Halliwell)
('*Pride of Race*,' Kenneth A. Wright)

1936 **Fodens Motor Works** (Fred Mortimer)
('*Kenilworth*,' Arthur Bliss)

1937 **Fodens Motor Works** (Fred Mortimer)
('*Pageantry*,' Herbert Howells)

1938 **Fodens Motor Works** (Fred Mortimer)
('*An Epic Symphony*,' Percy Fletcher)

1939–44 None

1945 **Fairey Aviation Works** (Harry Mortimer)
('*Overture for an Epic Occasion*,'
Denis Wright)

1946 **Brighouse & Rastrick** (Eric Ball)
('*Oliver Cromwell*,' Henry Geehl)

1947 **Black Dyke Mills** (Harry Mortimer)
('*Freedom,*' Hubert Bath)
1948 **Black Dyke Mills** (Harry Mortimer)
('*On the Cornish Coast,*' Henry Geehl)
1949 **Black Dyke Mills** (Harry Mortimer)
('*Comedy Overture,*' John Ireland)
1950 **Fodens Motor Works** (Harry Mortimer)
('*Pageantry,*' Herbert Howells)
1951 **Black Dyke Mills** (Alex Mortimer)
('*Epic Symphony,*' Percy Fletcher)
1952 **Fairey Aviation Works** (Harry Mortimer)
('*The Frogs of Aristophanes,*'
Sir Granville Bantock, arr. Frank Wright)
1953 **Fodens Motor Works** (Harry Mortimer)
('*Diadem of Gold,*' G. Bailey,
arr. Frank Wright)
1954 **Fairey Aviation Works** (Harry Mortimer)
('*Sovereign Heritage,*' J. Beaver,
arr. Frank Wright)
1955 **Munn & Felton's Works** (Harry Mortimer)
('*Blackfriars,*' Edric Cundell,
arr. Frank Wright)
1956 **Fairey Aviation Works** (Major George Wilcocks)
('*Festival Music,*' Eric Ball)
1957 **Munn & Felton's Works** (Stanley Boddington)
('*Variations for Brass Band,*'
R. Vaughan Williams)
1958 **Fodens Motor Works** (Rex Mortimer)
('*Variations on The Shining River,*'
Edmund Rubbra)
1959 **Black Dyke Mills** (Major George Wilcocks)
('*The King of Ys,*' Lalo,
arr. Frank Wright)
1960 **Munn & Felton's (Footwear)** (Stanley Boddington)
('*Three Figures,*' Herbert Howells)
1961 **Black Dyke Mills** (Major George Wilcocks)
('*Les Francs Juges,*' Berlioz,
arr. Frank Wright)
1962 **C.W.S. (Manchester)** (Alex Mortimer)
('*The Force of Destiny,*' Verdi,
arr. Frank Wright)
1963 **C.W.S. (Manchester)** (Alex Mortimer)
('*The Belmont Variations,*' Sir Arthur Bliss)

1964 **G.U.S. (Footwear)** (Stanley Boddington)
('*Variations on a Ninth*,' Gilbert Vinter)
1965 **Fairey Band** (Leonard Lamb)
('*Triumphant Rhapsody*,' Gilbert Vinter)
1966 **G.U.S. (Footwear)** (Stanley Boddington)
('*Le Carnaval Romain*,' Berlioz arr. Frank Wright)
1967 **Black Dyke Mills** (Geoffrey Brand)
('*Journey into Freedom*,' Eric Ball)
1968 **Brighouse & Rastrick** (Walter Hargreaves)
('*Prelude, The Mastersingers*,'
Wagner, arr. Frank Wright)
1969 **Brighouse & Rastrick** (Walter Hargreaves)
('*High Peak*,' Eric Ball)
1970 **Grimethorpe Colliery** (George Thompson)
('*Pride of Youth*,' Gordon Jacob)
1971 **Wingates Temperance** (Denis Smith)
('*Le Roi d'Ys*,' Lalo, arr. Frank Wright)
1972 **Black Dyke Mills** (Geoffrey Brand)
('*A Kensington Concerto*,' Eric Ball)
1973 **Brighouse & Rastrick** (James Scott)
('*Freedom*,' Hubert Bath)
1974 **Cory** (Major H. A. Kenney)
('*Fantasy for Brass Band*,' Malcolm Arnold)
1975 **Black Dyke Mills** (Major P. Parkes)
('*Un Vie de Matelot*,' Robert Farnon)
1976 **Black Dyke Mills** (Major P. Parkes)
('*Sinfonietta for Brass Band—The Wayfarer*,'
Eric Ball)
1977 **Black Dyke Mills** (Major Peter Parkes)
('*Connotations for Brass Band*,' Edward Gregson)
1978 **Yorkshire Imperial Metals** (Denis Carr)
('*Checkmate*,' Sir Arthur Bliss)
1979 **Black Dyke Mills** (Major Peter Parkes)
('*Volcano*,' Robert Simpson)

Second Section

1945 Camborne Town
1946 Pressed Steel Works
1947 Hetton Silver
1948 Markham Main Colliery
1949 Rhyl Silver

1950 Hoo Silver
1951 Lewis Merthyr Work's In
1952 Royston New Monck. Col. In
1953 British Legion (Oldham)
1954 Wharncliffe Silkstone Coll.
1955 Chapel-en-le-Frith Town
1956 Pontardulais Town
1957 Langley Prize
1958 Slaithwaite
1959 Kinneil Colliery
1960 Lindley
1961 Cammell Laird
1962 West Brom. Borough
1963 Skelmanthorpe
1964 Wellesley Colliery
1965 Mirrlees Works
1966 Cheetham Hill
1967 Snibston Colliery
1968 Haydock
1969 Thoresby Colliery
1970 Newhall
1971 Rogerstone & District
1972 Lockwood
1973 Tredegar Town
1974 Spillers (Gainsborough)
1975 Northumbria Police
1976 Loughborough
1977 Clacton-on-Sea
1978 Birmingham School of Music
1979 Leyland Vehicles

Third Section

1945 Houghton Main Colliery
1946 Mynyddygarreg Silver
1947 Rhos Silver
1948 Storeys of Lancaster
1949 British Legion (Oldham)
1950 Lewis Merthyr Work's In.
1951 John Dickinson (Apsley)
1952 Wharncliffe Silkstone Coll.
1953 Barnet

1954 Whitburn Miners' Welfare
1955 Pontardulais Town
1956 Walkden Prize
1957 Ellington Colliery
1958 Haigh Prize
1959 Steel Co. of Wales, Pt. Tal
1960 Rawmarsh Prize
1961 Paulton Silver
1962 Tadley Silver
1963 Poynton Brass
1964 Romford Civil Defence
1965 Sherborne Town
1966 Corby
1967 Rhymney Workmen's
1968 Pelton Fell Workmen's
1969 Teversal Colliery
1970 Cargo Fleet Works
1971 Redbridge Youth
1972 Wigan and District Brass
1973 Haworth
1974 Thornsett
1975 Wakefield Youth
1976 St. Keverne Silver
1977 Walsall Metropolitan
1978 Carlton Silver
1979 Corby Beanfield

Fourth Section

1947 Butterfield's Tank Works
1948 Wincanton Silver
1949 Gomersal Mills
1950 Kibworth Silver
1951 95th (Crewe) Sq. A.T.C.
1952 Ellington Colliery
1953 Ystalyfera Public
1954 Woodhorn Colliery
1955 Brancepeth Colliery
1956 Esh Colliery Welfare
1957 Gwaun-cae–Gurwen
1958 Elland Silver
1959 Cammell Laird Works

1960 Poynton Brass
1961 Hetton Silver Prize
1962 Corby Silver
1963 Cargo Fleet Works
1964 Stanhope Silver
1965 Guildford Silver
1966 Hatfield Main
1967 Chapeltown Silver
1968 Workington Town
1969 City of Coventry 'B'
1970 Harpenden
1971 Ebbw Vale Municipal
1972 Fishburn Colliery Welfare
1973 R.N.R. Dundee
1974 West Wycombe Brass
1975 North Skelton & District
1976 Queensbury Music Centre
1977 Hammonds Sauce 'B'
1978 Ecclesfield Silver
1979 Darwen

World Champions 1968–1971

1968 Brighouse & Rastrick (Walter Hargreaves)
(Prelude, '*The Mastersingers*,' Wagner-Frank
Wright)
1969 Brighouse & Rastrick (Walter Hargreaves)
('*High Peak*,' Eric Ball)
1970 Black Dyke Mills (Geoffrey Brand)
('*Benvenuto Cellini*,' Berlioz-Frank Wright)
1971 G.U.S. (**Footwear**) (Stanley Boddington)
('*Energy*,' Robert Simpson)

European Champions

1978 Black Dyke Mills (Major Peter Parkes)
('*Introduction, Elegy and Caprice*,'
Calvert and own choice)

1979 Black Dyke Mills (Major Peter Parkes)
('*Symphonic Music*,'
Hubert, and own choice).

Band enthusiast's diary

While every care has been taken to be as accurate as possible in compiling this list of annual events, it is possible that dates and venues may vary from year to year. No claim is laid to its being a complete list of events.

January

Rochdale, Lancashire, Annual Brass Band Festival
Northumberland Brass Band League contest
Gloucestershire annual solo and quartet contest

February

South West Festival, Barnstaple, Devon
Milton Keynes (Bucks) Brass Band Festival
Hammersmith, London, Own Choice contest, Hammersmith Town Hall
Wembley Winter Festival, Wembley Conference Centre
Oxford and District Brass Band Association annual winter contest
Yorkshire regional qualifying round, National championships, Bradford

March

Pontins Easter Festival
Lansing Bagnall Brass Band Festival, Basingstoke, Hants
Scottish championships and Scottish regional qualifying round, Falkirk
North West Brass Band Association championships
Cornwall Brass Band Association contest, Truro
Yorkshire area Mineworkers contest, Sheffield
Babycham Trophy brass band contest

151

Allendale Own Choice Contest, Workington, Cumbria
Alexander Owen Memorial Scholarship, Manchester
London and Southern Counties regional qualifying round, Watford, Herts
Northern regional qualifying round, Middlesbrough
North Western regional qualifying round, Preston
Wales regional qualifying round, Swansea

April

Nottingham Open Brass Band Contest
Yorkshire and Humberside Brass Band Association contest, York
East Anglian Brass Band Association Spring Contest, Thetford
Southern Counties Spring Contest
West of England regional qualifying round, National championships, Bristol
Midlands regional qualifying round, Derby

May

Spring Festival, Belle Vue, Manchester
Pontins Spring Own Choice Contest
East Anglian Entertainment Contest, Great Yarmouth
Weston-super-Mare annual contest
Wessex annual summer festival, Weymouth
Whit Friday Quickstep contests, Stalybridge, etc

June

West of England Bandsmens' Festival, Bugle, Cornwall
Welsh Miners' Gala contest, Cardiff
Scottish Miners' Gala contest, Edinburgh
Northumberland Miners' Gala contest, Bedlington

August

Edinburgh annual invitation brass band contest
Welsh National Eisteddfod
Morecambe brass band contest

September

British Open Championship, Belle Vue, Manchester
Clacton-on-Sea, Essex, Band Festival
Royal Leamington Spa Brass Band Festival

October

National Championships, Royal Albert Hall, London (and adjoining centres)
Butlin's Youth Championships, Royal Albert Hall
European Championships, Royal Albert Hall
Oldham Brass Band Entertainment contest
Folkestone (Kent) annual brass band contest

November

Mineworkers' National Festival, Blackpool
Rothman Brass in Concert championships, Darlington
City of Leicester annual brass band festival
Pontins Championships Finals, Prestatyn, Clwyd
Reading Brass Band Guild annual contest and concert
Northern Ireland championships, Belfast
Annual Quartet and Solo championship, Oxford
Watford (Herts) annual contest
South West Brass Band Association annual contest, Paignton, Devon
London and Home Counties Brass Band Association annual championships

December

Tyne and Wear Brass Band Contest, Newcastle
North West Leicestershire solo and quartet contest
Wessex Brass Band Association annual festival, Bournemouth

Appendix Four

Discography

The following list contains some of the many brass band records available. It does not attempt to be fully comprehensive but does include many of the latest records available. Catalogues of brass band recordings can be obtained from a number of specialist suppliers, including:

Chandos Music Ltd,
41 Charing Cross Road,
London WC2 OAR

Studio Music Co.,
77-79 Dudden Hill Lane,
London NW10 1BD

R. Smith and Co. Ltd,
P.O. Box 210,
Watford, Herts.
WD2 4YG

Wright and Round Ltd,
Pickford Buildings,
Parliament Street,
Gloucester GL1 1HY.

Grosvenor Records,
10 Grosvenor Road,
Birmingham B20 3NP

Salvation Army
Publishing and Supplies Department,
Judd Street,
London WC1

Besses o' th' Barn Band

Grosvenor GRS 1042	Viva Vivaldi; Swedish Rhapsody; Windmills from Amsterdam; Hora Staccato; Sonata for Horn and Band; Rock of Ages; the Plantagenets.
Pye TB 3012	*English Brass*; Moorside Suite; A Dales Suite; Downland Suite; Solitude.
Pye TB 3016	*English Brass - Vol. 2* Severn Suite; Canzon Duodecimi Toni; Variations for Brass Band; Chromascope.
Chandos BBR 1002	*Besses in Australia* Iolanthe Overture; David of the White Rock; Dublin's Fair City; Annie Laurie; Famous British Marches; Australian Fantasy; Colonial Song; Down Under; Zanette.

Black Dyke Mills Band

Pye GH 632	*Golden Hour of Black Dyke Mills* Crown Imperial; Londonderry Air; Napoli; Challenging Brass; Little Suite for Brass No. 1; Finlandia; The Contestor; Where e'er you walk; Journey into Freedom; Elizabethan Serenade; Pandora; The Lost Chord.
RCA RS 1083	*A Christmas Fantasy* (with Huddersfield Choral Society). We wish you a Merry Christmas; a Christmas Festival Overture; Nativity Carol; God Rest ye Merry Gentlemen; Farandole; The Shepherds' Farewell; Ring Out Wild Bells; For unto us a child is born; Shepherd's Hey; The Twelve Days of Christmas; O come all ye faithful; Sussex Carol; A Christmas Fantasy.
RCA PL 25117	*European Brass* (with Edward Heath). Polka (Bartered Bride); Thievish Magpie; Rusalka's Song to the Moon; Entry of the Hunters; Miniature Overture; Siciliana and Giga; Rhapsody on Sea Shanties; Morning Cloud; Pomp and Circumstance No. 1.
RCA PL 25078	*British Music for Brass Bands* Severn Suite; Variations on 'The Shining River'; Epic Symphony; The Wayfarer.
RCA PL 25089	*The Lion and the Eagle* Yeoman of the Guard; Phil the Fluter's Ball; Land of my Fathers; Finale from Suite No 2 (Holst); A Scottish Lament; Pomp and Circumstance

No 4; Stars and Stripes; Rhapsody on Negro Spirituals; A Stephen Foster Fantasy; A George Gershwin Medley.

RCA
PL 25143

Triple Champions Connotations; Diadem of Gold; Vivat Regina (Mathias); Harmonious Variations of a Theme of Handel (Langford).

Chandos

BBR 1001

Black Dyke Plays Wings Mull of Kintyre; Band on the Run; Love Awake; Let 'em in; Big Barn Bed; With a Little Luck; London Town; Jet; My Love; Listen to What the Man said.

Brighouse and Rastrick Band

Grosvenor
GRS 1035

Mosaic for Band Overture Provence; Chanson de Matin; Passacaglia from Concerto for Trombone and Brass Band; Toccata from Suite Gothique; Mosaic; Solemn Melody; Farandole from L'Arlesienne.

Grosvenor
GRS 1050

(With Don Lusher). Concert Variations; Cornets A Go-Go; Almost a Lullaby; Harlem Nocturne; Battle Hymn of the Republic; Making Whoopee; In the Wee Small Hours of the Morning; Phil the Fluter's Ball; The Trombone Men; Mood Indigo; The Typewriter.

Logo
1001

The Floral Dance Lincolnshire Poacher; Lara's Theme; Tijuana Tuba; Zambesi; Solitaire; The Floral Dance; Bachelor Girls; Try to Remember; African Waltz; Scarborough Fair; Theme from Shaft; Strawberry Fair.

EMI
NTS 147

Barwick Green Barwick Green; A North Countrie Fantasy; The Dover Coach; Theme from 'The Forsyte Saga'; Cornish Cavalier; Entry of the Gladiators; Trojan March; Caprice and Variations on a theme of Arban; The Buccaneer; French Military March.

Carlton Main Frickley Colliery Band

Grosvenor
GRS 1020

Labour and Love Overture to the Arcadians; Fire – Star Polka; Hyfordol; Labour and Love; Nibelungen March; Aurelia; Romance from the Fair Maid of Perth; To a Wild Rose; Funeral March for a Marionette; Cornet Carillon; Mephistopheles Contest March.

Grosvenor GRS 1043	*Life Divine* March, BB and CF; Land of the Mountain and the Flood; Polka, Shylock; Bobby's Tune; Sunset; Serenade from 'Les Millions d' Arlequin'; Hymn tune, St Clements; Life Divine.
Decca SB 339	Signature March: F.C.B.; Fingals Cave; Serenade for Trombone; Waltz from Masquerade; Hunting Polka; Processional March from Caractacus; Gay Gnu; Streets of London; Epic Theme.

City of Coventry Band

Grosvenor GRS 1053	*Spirit of Pageantry* Fandango Asturianna; Zelda; March of the Pacemakers; Overture for an Epic Occasion; Intermezzo from Karelia; Fanfare and Soliloquy.
Decca SB 332	*Sounds of Brass Series* Trumpet Spectacular; Dubinushka; Love's Enchantment; New World Symphony; Tintagel; Bell Bird Polka; Marche Heroique; Sundown.
Pye TB 3019	*City of Coventry Band: Celebration of its 40th Anniversary* Fest Musik Der Stadt Wien; The Watermill; Mexican March; The Lark in the Clear Air; Gopak; Symphonic study: The Line of Life; The Blaze of Light; The Swan; March of the Toys; Adagio from Concierto de Aranjuez; Solveig's Song and Anitra's Dance; Toccata Marziale.

Cory Band

Grosvenor GRS 1052	*Salute to the New World* Rule Britannia; Chorale and Rock-out; Elegy from Epic Symphony; Dashing Away with a Smoothing Iron; Manhattan Beach; Jeannie; Marche des Bouffons; Largo from New World Symphony; Fantasia on the Dargason.
Decca SB 319	*Sounds of Brass Series* Fantasy for Brass; Cotswold Lullaby; Carambina; Allegro Preciso; Waltz with a Beat; Hootennany; Slavonic Dance; Believe me, if all those endearing young charms; Latin-Americana; Marriage of Figaro.
Decca SB 340	Aces High; Myfanwy; Rule Britannia; Symphony of Marches (Vinter); March, Opus 99 (Prokofiev); Y Deryn Pur; The Blue and the Gray; Miller Moods.

C.W.S. (Manchester) Band

Decca
SB 309

Sounds of Brass Series Thundercrest; Serenade; Plaisir D'Amour; Night on the Bare Mountain; Crown Imperial; Night of Gladness; Two Preludes (Chopin); The Nightingale; Rule Britannia.

William Davis Construction Group Band

Virtuosi
R 7910

Spring Collection Cornish Cavalier; I Don't Know How to Love Him; Cushy Butterfield; Sinfonietta; The Great Gate of Kiev; Pink Panther; All Through the Night; MacArthur Park; 12th Street Rag.

Desford Colliery Band

Decca
SB 335

Something Old, Something New Fanfare for the Common Man; Overture Zampa; A requiem Chorus; Feelings; Don Quixote; Exhibition Can-Can; Who Pays the Ferryman; Cornet Solo; Zelda; Finlandia.

Ever Ready Band

Decca
SB 329

Sounds of Brass Series. High Command; Crimond; Theme and Variations (Hummel); Salute to Youth; North. Country Fantasie; Romanza for Euphonium; Severn Suite.

Decca
SB 334

Sounds of Brass series. March of the Bowmen; Selection, Cavalleria Rusticana; Largo from 'Xerxes'; Thunder and Lightning Polka; Neapolitan Suite for Brass; Russian Dance; Concerto for Two Trumpets; Finale themes from Symphony No. 5 (Tchaikovsky).

Dansan
DS 017

Stars of the North Fest Musik der Stadt Wien; Cushy Butterfield; Lark in the Clear Air; Simon Called Peter; Reflections for Brass; Hunting the Hare; Blaze of Light; Cock o' th' North; Cavatina; Homage March; Sleepy Serenade; Star Wars

Fairey Engineering Band

BBC Records REC 302	*Champion Brass* King Cotton; Perpetuum Mobile; Send in the Clowns; Introduction to Act 3 Lohengrin; The Girl I left behind me; If; Round the Clock; Queen of Sheba; Can-Can; Don't Cry for me Argentina; Polly-Wolly Doodling; Hustle; Peace; Fanfare and Soliloquy.
Decca SB 304	*Sounds of Brass series* Radetzky march; Morning from Peer Gynt; Buffoon; Festival Overture; Headless Horseman; Beaufighters March; Prelude Act 1, La Traviata; Father and I; The Hunt.
Decca SB 318	*Sounds of Brass series* More Concert Classics. Flight of the Bumble bee; L'Italiana in Algeri; Chorus of Hebrew Slaves from Nabucco; Children's Overture; Sonata Pian E Forte; Polonaise from Christmas Night; Moorside Suite.
EMI NTS 167	*A Souvenir of Memories* Marching with Sousa; Serenade from String Quartet in F; Oh! My Beloved Father; Waltz, Donnauwellen; The Three Musketeers; Radetzky March; Romanza; Andante Cantabile; Symphonic poem, Les Preludes.

Fodens Motor Works Band

Decca SB 330	*Sounds of Brass series* Nibelungen March; Blow the Wind Southerly; Silver threads among the gold; Things to Come; Fantasia on British Airs; Prelude from 'The Talisman'; La Sonnambula; March Slav.
Decca SB 333	*Sounds of Brass series* Prelude and Fuge; The Sea; Thalassa; Melody and Caprice; Bees-A-Buzzin'; Semper Fidelis; Overture from Die Fliedermaus; Intermezzo from Patterns in Brass; March and Trepak from Casse Noisette Suite; La Reine de Saba.

G.U.S. (Footwear) Band

EMI OW 2159	*Kings of Brass* Out of the Blue; Spanish Gypsy Dance; Carnaval Romain; Espana; Sons of the Brave; Angelus; R.A.F. March Past; Estudiantina; Samum; Bells Across

the Meadow; An American Patrol; New Colonial March.

Encore   *Championship Bandstand* Includes items and solos dat-
ONCR 514   ing from 1959 to 1965, with the 1972 performance of
                James Cook – Circumnavigator.

Polyphonic   *Quartets for Brass* Elegy and Rondo; Fancy's Knell;
PRL 003   Alla Burlesca; Lully's March; Purcell's Song; Rameau's
                Tambourin; Handel's Air; Bach's Badinerie; Corelli's
                Dance; Couperin's Lullaby; Loeilly's Jig.

Grimethorpe Colliery Band

Decca   *Sounds of Brass series* Red Sky at Night; Hogarth's Hoe
SB 325   Down; I Dream of Jeannie; Barney's Tune; Cornet Con-
                certo; Chinese Take-Away; Parade; Paris le soir; Mos-
                aic; Stars and Stripes.

Decca   *Classics for Brass Band* Moorside Suite; Comedy Ov-
SXL 6820   erture; Severn Suite; Kenilworth.

Decca   Grimethorpe Special.
Head 14   Fireworks; Garden Rain; Grimethorpe Aria; Ragtimes
                and Habaneras.

RCA   *Band of the Year* March, NYBBS; Lark in the Clear
PL 25048   Air; Sleeping Beauty Waltz; Cleopatra; Sarie Marais;
                March from Suite No 1 (Holst); Overture on Famous
                English Airs; Intermezzo from Cavaleria Rusticana;
                Trumpet Voluntary; Variations on a theme of Lully.

Hammonds Sauce Works Band

Pye   *Super Quality Plus* Quality Plus; Cornet solo Cleopatra;
GSGL 10455   Nimrod; Fra Diavolo Overture; The Gladiator; Eu-
                phonium solo, Non Piu Andrai (Marriage of Figaro);
                Abide with Me; Carnival in Paris

Pye   *Yorkshire Brass* Comedians' Gallop; Carnival of Ven-
GSGL 10494   ice; Zorba's Dance; The Acrobat; Miller Magic; The
                Miniature (cornet solo); Beguine for Brass; Chanson
                Indoue; Il Turco in Italia.

Polyphonic PRL 001	*Spectacular Brass* Brass Spectacular; None Shall Sleep; Tijuana Holiday; Dance Hongroise; Caprice; Skyline; Mellow Mood; Blades of Toledo; Elvira Madigan Theme; Slavonic Dance No 1 (Dvořák).

Kilmarnock Concert Brass

Louden Records LDN 470 Available from Louden Records, 15 Main Street, Strathaven, Scotland.	March of the Pacemakers; My Love is like a red, red rose; The Hustle; Aurelia; Blaydon Races; Chanson D'Amour; Pageantry; Romance from the Fair Maid of Perth; Onward Christian Soldiers; Hootennany.

Leyland Vehicles Band

RCA PL 25175	*Travelling with Leyland* Royal Tiger; The Dover Coach; The Slow Train; Perpetuum Mobile; Coronation Scot; Titan March; Daisy Bell; Sailing; Concorde March; Those Magnificent Men in their Flying Machines; Tam O'Shanter's Ride.

Mirrlees Works Band

Grosvenor GRS 1069	*Snapshots* Bandology; Rule Britannia; The Nightingale; Napoleon Galop; Whitehall; Portuguese Party; I Don't Know how to Love Him; Swedish Rhapsody; Blaydon Races; Plymouth Hoe.

Morris Concert Band

Meridian A22001 Available from Boosey & Hawkes, Ltd., 295 Regent Street, London W1	*Brass Tacks* On Parade; Runaway Rocking Horse; Bell Bird Polka; Echo de Bastion; Cairngorm Patrol; Away Lifeboat; The Trombone Men; Sky Watch; Second Thoughts; Wonder March; March from 'A Little Suite'; Overture to Prince Igor.

Morris Motors Band

Polyphonic   *Marching Contrasts*   Marche Militaire-La Ronde; Oh,
PRL 002   Listen to the Band; Bally Castle Bay; Mancunian Way;
The Queen's Trumpeters; The St John March; Semper
Sousa; By Royal Command; Bugle Call Blues; The
Rover's Return; The Duke of York's Patrol; Corner
Flag; The European; Seventy Six Trombones.

Parc and Dare Band

Decca   *Sounds of Brass series*   March of the Peers; Cornet
SB 336   Roundabout; Black Magic Woman; I Wish You Love;
Suite for Brass; Hob Y Derri Dando; MacArthur
March; Tuba Tapestry; A Horseman Riding By; Con-
certino for Tenor Horn and Band; Chorale and
Rockout.

Rochdale Band

Grosvenor   *The Crusaders*   March, Bramwyn; Euphonium solo,
GRS 1054   Robin Adair; Symphonic Rhapsody, The Crusaders;
Trombone trio, The Swing of the Scale; Hymn tune,
Deep Harmony; Gypsy Rondo; Cornet solo, I Hear You
Calling Me; Overture, Two Blind Men of Toledo.

Sun Life Stanshawe Band

Decca   *Sounds of Brass series*   Thievish Magpie; Hava Nagila;
SB 322   Berceuse de Jocelyn; Tchaikovsky's 5th Symphony;
Gold and Silver; Polka from Bartered Bride;
Grandfather's Clock; Frogs of Aristophanes.

Two-Ten   *Oliver Cromwell*   Rosslyn; Prestbury Park; Tuba Tap-
TT 001   estry; Concert Overture, the Prizewinners; Oliver
Cromwell; Fantasy for Tuba; Rock of Ages.

Saydisc   Spectrum; Variations on a Ninth; Academic Festival
SOLB 262   Overture; Suite Gothique.

RCA   *Langford in Concert*   Carnival Day; Scarborough Fair;
PL 25185   Caller Herrin; The Seventies Set; Softly Awakes My
Heart; Widdecombe Fair; Salute to the Six; Cushy But-

terfield; Après un Rêve (Fauré); A West Country Fantasy; The Boy from Menaem; Metropolis.

Wingates Temperance Band

Grosvenor
GRS 1045

Fireworks and Sparklers The Lost Chord; Fireworks; The Thunderer; Meditation from Thais; Winter Dreams; Finale from Capriccio Espagnol.

Decca
SB 338

Sounds of Brass series Peace and War; Glenn Miller Special; The Shadow of Your Smile; Finale from Tchaikovsky Symphony No 4; Soldiers' Chorus from Faust; Trumpeters' Holiday; Elegy from Suite for Brass Band; Solitaire; Themes from Jesus Christ Superstar.

Yorkshire Imperial Metals Band

Pye
GSGL 10488

Highlights in Brass Prelude for an Occasion; Festival Music; Bandology; Rhapsody in Blue; Rondo from 4th horn concerto; American Patrol; Una Voce Poco Fa.

Two-Ten
TT 002

Glemdene; Napoli; Peasants Song; Scene Sinfonica; Concert Prelude; Rhapsody for Eb Soprano Cornet; Portsmouth; Berceuse; Strand-on-the-Green.

Two-Ten
TT 003

Checkmate County Palatine; Two of the Tops; Serenade; Tam O' Shanter's Ride; March, Yorkshire Imperial; Fantasy for Euphonium; Panorama (Sleeping Beauty); Dances from Checkmate.

National Brass Band Festival

RCA
PL 25118

1977 Grimethorpe Colliery, Stanshawe, Wingates Temperance, Yorkshire Imperial Metals with Gerard Schwarz.
Orb and Sceptre; Greensleeves; Berne March; Finale from Concerto No 2 (Bourgeois); Introduction, Act III Lohengrin; Life Divine; Trumpet Voluntary; Concerto for Trumpet; Russlan and Ludmilla.

RCA
PL 25192

1978 Carlton Main Frickley Colliery, Ever Ready, Great Universal and Besses O' Th' Barn Bands, with Black Dyke Mills Band, Solna Brass, Don Lusher and his Trombone Ensemble. October Festival; Caribbean Cameo; Alla Marcia Serenade for Strings; Rhapsody in Brass; European Fantasy; Lincolnshire Poacher; The Hall of the Mountain King; The Corsair; March Slav.

Chandos
BBR 1003

1979 Besses o' th' Barn, Parc and Dare, Hammonds Sauce Works, Sun Life Stanshawe and Wingates Temperance, with Brighouse and Rastrick, James Shepherd Versatile Brass and Michael Lind (tuba). Homage March; Toccata and Fugue in D Minor (Bach); Symphonic Study; Festmusik der Stadt Wien; Carnival Day; Foxtrot Between Friends; Blue Rondo a la Turk; Pandora; Carnival of Venice; Strauss Fantasy.

Miscellaneous

EMI
NTS 145

A Lifetime of Music Harry Mortimer's All-Star Brass. Mephistopheles; The Arcadians; Passing By; Grandfather's Clock; Sandon; Death or Glory; Marche Militaire; The Tops; March of the Manikins; No, No, Nanette; Tea for Two; Love will find a way; She will say her say; The Robber's Chorus; Farandole from L'Arlesienne.

RCA
PL 25147

Swedish Champions Solna Brass. Alla Marcia; Norwegian Dance No 2; Maple Leaf Rag; Valse Triste; Spanish Gypsy Dance; Old Fadopsalm; Under the Blue and Yellow Flag; Trombone Concerto; Mock Morris; Second Swedish Rhapsody.

Pendulum
9109 701

Skellern, featuring Grimethorpe Colliery Band You and I; When I Got You; Big 'G'; 'T's All 'Cos o' You; While I'm Away; Love is the Sweetest Thing; Sweet Words; When Somebody Thinks You're Wonderful; Put Out the Flame; Where Do We Go From Here.

Chandos
SCM 1003

Champion Bands of Europe Brass Band 'De Waldsang'. Glemdene; The Mill on the Cliff; Challenge; John O' Gaunt; The Boy from Manaem; Eye Level; Mexico Grandstand; Feelings; Floral Dance; Trumpet Fiesta; Black Magic Woman.

Pye
GH 662

Golden Hour series Themes in Brass. Various Championship Bands. Colditz March; Eye Level; The Devil's Gallop; Theme from a New World; The Entertainer;

Clayhanger; Moon River; Jaws; Swedish Rhapsody; Star Wars; Zorba's Dance; The Duchess of Duke Street; Entry of the Gladiators; Summertime; Who Pays the Ferry Man; Air from Suite in D; Godspell – Jesus Christ Superstar Medley.

EMI
NTS 157

Sailing from the Clyde Greenock and District Silver Band, with the choir of St Michael's Academy, Kilwinning. The Contestor; Clydeoscope Medley; Stranger on the Shore; Sailing; Betty Dear; Jesus Christ Superstar; Men of Harlech; Hawaii Five-O; Scots Wha'Ha'e; My Love is like a Red, Red Rose; Frolic for Trombones; Bramwyn.

Two-Ten
TTV 099

Vintage Brass St Hilda Colliery, Black Dyke Mills, Foden's Motor Works with soloists, Harry Mortimer (cornet), Jack Mackintosh (cornet), Alex Mortimer (euphonium) and Jack Pinches (trombone) in recordings of the 1920s and 1930s.

Salvation Army

SAC 5077   *Brass Band Festival* International Staff Band.

SXOP 50015 *Brass Impact* International Staff Band.

Banners and
Bonnets
BAB 3502

City Tempo International Staff Band.

Banners and
Bonnets
BAB 3512

With One Accord International Staff Band; Melbourne Staff Band and New York Staff Band.

Banners and
Bonnets
BAB 3519

Symphony of Praise International Staff Band, Melbourne Staff Band and New York Staff Band.

Banners and
Bonnets
BAB 3510

Celebration Kettering Citadel Band. Exodus (Ball); Euphonium solo, Home on the Range.

Banners and
Bonnets
BAB 3513

All Things Bright and Beautiful Upper Norwood SA Band, with Michael Clack (organ). A collection of 23 hymns and songs.

Banners and Bonnets BAB 3514	*Marching to Glory* Portsmouth Citadel Band and the Band of the Salvation Army National School of Music. The Wellingtonian; In the King's Service; Salute to America; Bognor Regis; Motondo; Hadleigh Camp; Victors Acclaimed; Victorious; Mighty to Save; Long Point; Silver Star; Collaroy; Crown of Conquest; Petone Citadel; Brooklyn Citadel.
Banners and Bonnets BAB 3516	*My Strength, My Tower* Enfield Citadel Band. Festival March, Crusaders; Cornet solo, Tucker; Rhapsodic Variations, My Strength, My Tower; The Redcliffe March; Selection, the Children's Friend; Selection, Wells of Gladness; Meditation, How Charming is Thy Name.

Index

167